T0194181

SECOND EDITION

Smart Kids
with Learning Difficulties

SECOND EDITION

Smart Kids

with Learning
Difficulties

**OVERCOMING OBSTACLES
AND REALIZING POTENTIAL**

Rich Weinfeld, Linda Barnes-Robinson,
Sue Jeweler, & Betty Roffman Shevitz

Routledge
Taylor & Francis Group

NEW YORK AND LONDON

DEDICATION

To all of the bright students who struggle in school and their parents and teachers who are dedicated to helping them discover their true gifts and talents. We also dedicate this book to our families—our parents, siblings, spouses, children, and grandchildren.

Library of Congress Cataloging-in-Publication Data

Smart kids with learning difficulties : overcoming obstacles and realizing potential /
by Rich Weinfeldby, Linda Barnes-Robinson, Sue Jeweler, & Betty Roffman Shevitz.
-- Second edition
    pages cm
 Includes bibliographical references.
 ISBN 978-1-61821-076-0 (pbk.)
1. Learning disabled children--Education--United States. 2. Gifted children--
Education--United States. 3. Special education--United States. I. Weinfeld, Rich,
1953-
 LC4705.S615 2013
 371.9--dc23
                                2013016138
First published in 2013 by Prufrock Press Inc.

Published in 2021 by Routledge
605 Third Avenue, New York, NY 10017
2 Park Square, Milton Park, Abingdon, Oxon OX14 4RN

Routledge is an imprint of the Taylor & Francis Group, an informa business

Copyright © 2013 by Taylor & Francis Group

Cover and layout design by Raquel Trevino

ISBN: 9781032144283(hbk)
ISBN: 9781618210760(pbk)

DOI: 10.4324/9781003237983

CONTENTS

ACKNOWLEDGEMENTS

For the second edition of our book, we pay tribute to the young men and women who are making significant contributions to our lives in the 21st century, for these are some of our former students whom we first met some 20–30 years ago as we embarked on our own journeys to support and provide programming for these extraordinary young people. We also acknowledge their parents who were there every step of the way.

In the beginning, there was Waveline Starnes who inspired and guided us. Then, there was the compassion and support of Virginia Tucker. There was the wisdom and clarity of thinking of Joyce VanTassel-Baska. And, finally, there was the expertise and leadership of Susan Baum. We are grateful and honored to have known and worked with these four extraordinary women who have dedicated their professional lives to providing challenging programs for all students.

We also acknowledge all of the pioneers in this field whose work has provided the basis for much of our knowledge of who these kids are and what works for them, and to the teachers who have made it happen in their classrooms every day, especially Lois Baldwin, Mary Preston, Martha Abolins, Larry March, Marisa Stemple, and Dennis Higgins.

Introduction

Parents and teachers alike have responded enthusi-astically since the 2006 publication of the original *Smart Kids With Learning Difficulties*. The feedback received has been both instructive and heartwarming. For the teach-ers who asked for many more specific strategies and tools that they could use in their classrooms with their students and in their communication with parents, the 2011 book, *101 School Success Tools for Smart Kids With Learning Dif-ficulties*, by Shevitz, Stemple, Barnes-Robinson, and Jew-eler was published. For the parents who asked us for more hands-on ideas and materials to use with their children, as well as more current updates in the field during the past 8 years, this updated and expanded edition of *Smart Kids With Learning Difficulties* shares the most recent research and information.

DOI:10.4324/9781003237983-1

This revised edition follows the same format and topic organization as the first edition. There is a new feature provided at the end of each chapter—a summary of the Key Points found within the chapters—that will help focus and facilitate next steps and desired follow-up for parents and teachers.

Diamonds are rare. Two-hundred and fifty tons of rock, sand, and gravel must be processed to yield one carat of polished diamond. The diamonds we will be discussing are also rare. Bright students with learning difficulties are often not identified because their brilliance and roughness may mask one another. We see only the rough parts, such as their inability to write or read effectively. What results is an attitude of discouragement and defeat. When we do find these diamonds, we must help them to shine and reach their potential by identifying their gifts and talents.

Every day, parents and teachers are challenged to find ways to empower their bright kids who, while able to participate actively in a class discussion, may be unable to write a complete sentence. They are the students who rarely have homework completed, or if done, cannot find it. They may be light-years ahead in math, but reading below grade level. In contrast, these same students are the ones who may not only be able to program the computer, but completely take it apart and put it back together again. Ask them about dinosaurs, global warming, lasers, or ancient civilizations and you might get bombarded with information, but ask them to write about the same topic and they may produce little or nothing. Ask a smart student with learning difficulties to write a research paper on bridges, and he may be unable to complete the assignment. However, sitting on a table at home may be an elaborate structure this same student has built out of LEGOs™ or toothpicks that reflects his understanding of advanced concepts in physics, engineering, and architecture. Outside of class, these students are the creative problem solvers and analytical thinkers who show strong task commitment when the topic is personally meaningful. In school, frustrated by their inability to demonstrate academic achievement commensurate with their ability, they often have feelings of inadequacy and are at great risk of failing.

Students who are bright and underachieving, including those who are gifted and talented/learning disabled (GT/LD), must be given access to rigorous and challenging instruction. Accommodating for a student's learning disabilities or difficulties is essential. Dynamic tools can empower smart kids with learning difficulties to access appropriate instruction using their strengths while improving and working around their weaknesses.

The purpose of *Smart Kids With Learning Difficulties: Overcoming Obstacles and Realizing Potential* is to guide parents and educators toward identifying and planning for these bright, underachieving kids so that they will reach their true potential. This book deals with research and experience the authors have gained from working directly with students who are smart, but have problems in school. We believe that the learning and teaching methods that have been applied successfully to both the gifted and talented and the learning disabled populations can, and should, be used with all bright kids with learning difficulties, whether they have official labels or not.

This book is divided into five chapters that answer the following questions:

- Who are these kids?
- How do we find them?
- What needs to be done, and who is responsible for doing it?
- What do good programs and services look like?
- What actions ensure that our bright kids will overcome their learning difficulties?

Navigating an educational system can be a challenge. A Road Map (like the one provided on p. 8) gives a visual representation of the direction that parents and educators may follow to ensure that a student will access appropriate services.

At the end of each chapter in this book is a collection of reproducible tools for parents, teachers, and students to use. They are designed to help ensure that the needs of our bright underachieving kids are met. The TIPS (To Impact Pupil Success) that appear for each tool suggest how a parent, educator, or student can utilize these supplementary materials effectively.

We suggest you enlarge these tools on a copy machine and use them as part of your day-to-day interactions with smart students who face learning challenges.

When using this book and the reproducible tools within it, we suggest you:

- read the book to gain a deeper understanding of the law, population characteristics, identification, guiding principles for success, interventions, programs and services, and the actions necessary to ensure success for bright underachieving students;
- use the Road Map for assistance when navigating educational systems;
- use the book as you would a resource book, determining what information is applicable to your individual child;
- copy and use the applicable information and specific reproducible pages to help you ensure that the needs of your student are being addressed;
- give copies of appropriate information and tools to all parties involved—yourself, your child, and your child's school;
- use and create plans of action to implement successful instructional opportunities, programs, and services for your child;
- use the information as a jumping off point for further exploration on a subtopic of special interest; and
- use the reproducible pages to assist you with preparation and participation in both instructional opportunities and meetings and conferences.

TIPS AND TOOLS

Supplementary Materials

The pages following each chapter are designed to help ensure that the needs of our bright kids with learning difficulties are met. The TIPS (To Impact Pupil Success) that appear for each tool suggest how a parent, educator, or student can use the materials effectively. In addition, some of the material within the book's text has been reproduced in easy-to-use checklists, forms, and charts to satisfy a variety of learning styles and to provide you with a quick guide to the information you need to know.

Included in this section:

➢ Road Map

Road Map

What actions will ensure that our bright kids will overcome their learning difficulties? Use the Road Map (see p. 8) to see the big picture to find out where you are; where you are going; and how to get there when using this book, working to meet your child's needs, and navigating the school system.

Parents and teachers should work as partners in the process of identifying bright kids with learning difficulties and creating programming for them. This Road Map is designed so that it may be applied to your child or student. Each question and graphic on the flowchart is addressed in detail within the specific cited chapter in this book.

TIPS

Teacher

Use the Road Map for identifying appropriate resources within your school system and pinpointing potential steps for meeting students' needs.

Parent

The Road Map offers a look at the big picture. Use it to navigate your child's school system. Contact the appropriate school and district personnel whenever you need help with identification procedures, interventions, programs and services, and appropriate placement for your child. Use it in conjunction with this book to find out where you are in the process and where you need to go to help your child succeed.

Student

Use the Road Map with your parents and teachers to get the help you need when you need it.

The Road Map progresses from when you initially observe that a child has learning difficulties, to identification procedures, to programming and services decisions that need to be made, to placement in the best school setting possible, and other actions that ensure success.

The ultimate destination is a place that offers kids strength-based instruction, appropriate adaptations and accommodations, and an environment that empowers students to be successful.

An asterisk (*) on the Road Map signifies the appropriate place for the implementation of any/all of the following tools and strategies (refer to Chapter 3 for more information):

- best practices,
- guiding principles,
- strength-based instruction,
- adaptations or accommodations,
- overcoming obstacles,
- what works and what doesn't work,
- talent development (mentor), and
- roles and responsibilities.

Road Map

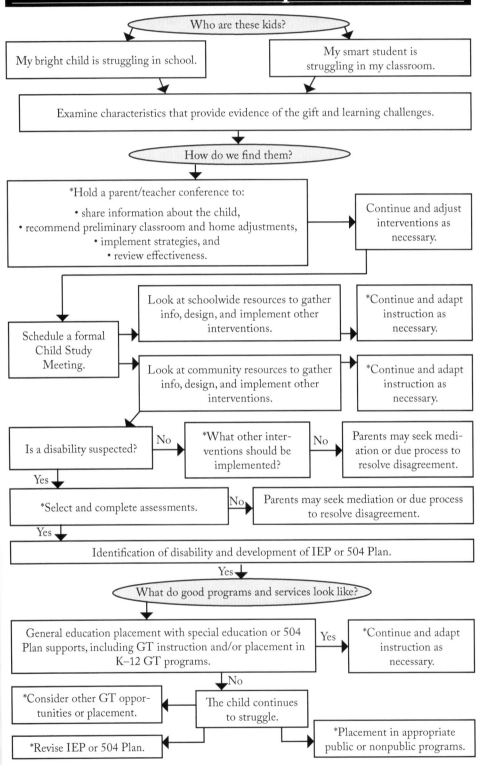

Who are these kids?

My bright child is struggling in school.

My smart student is struggling in my classroom.

Examine characteristics that provide evidence of the gift and learning challenges.

How do we find them?

*Hold a parent/teacher conference to:
- share information about the child,
- recommend preliminary classroom and home adjustments,
- implement strategies, and
- review effectiveness.

Continue and adjust interventions as necessary.

Schedule a formal Child Study Meeting.

Look at schoolwide resources to gather info, design, and implement other interventions.

*Continue and adapt instruction as necessary.

Look at community resources to gather info, design, and implement other interventions.

*Continue and adapt instruction as necessary.

Is a disability suspected? → No → *What other interventions should be implemented? → No → Parents may seek mediation or due process to resolve disagreement.

Yes ↓

*Select and complete assessments. → No → Parents may seek mediation or due process to resolve disagreement.

Yes ↓

Identification of disability and development of IEP or 504 Plan.

Yes ↓

What do good programs and services look like?

General education placement with special education or 504 Plan supports, including GT instruction and/or placement in K–12 GT programs. → Yes → *Continue and adapt instruction as necessary.

No ↓

The child continues to struggle.

*Consider other GT opportunities or placement.

*Placement in appropriate public or nonpublic programs.

*Revise IEP or 504 Plan.

Smart Kids With Learning Difficulties © Taylor & Francis Group

1

WHO ARE THESE KIDS?

Some kids struggle. Their backgrounds, socioeconomic conditions, strengths and needs, abilities and disabilities, and their journey through life may vary, but they all struggle with learning. Some, as the following vignettes show, win the struggle and become successful individuals who make extraordinary contributions to the world.

He was from an upper middle class family. His mother was musically inclined and his father was an engineer. He was a very quiet child who did not speak until age 3. He hated school and disliked authority. He did poorly with rote learning. His teachers said he was a slow learner who would never amount to anything. Later, he became interested in science, math, and electrical engineering,

 DOI:10.4324/9781003237983-2

but failed the exam for entry into an engineering program. Because of his interest in abstract and mathematical thought, he thought about becoming a teacher. However, he believed he lacked imagination and practical ability. His name was Albert Einstein, the famous mathematician and physics genius.

She came from a socially prominent family. Her father was an alcoholic and she lived with her maternal grandparents. She had little affection for her mother who called her "Granny" because of her appearance. She was sickly, bedridden, hospitalized often, and wore a back brace due to a spinal defect. She bit her nails, had phobias, was shy, felt rejected and ugly, craved praise and attention, was insecure, and had deep feelings of inadequacy. A daydreamer, she often preferred to be isolated. After many years in school, she began to exhibit leadership qualities. She proved to be altruistic and wanted to help the elderly and poor. Her name was Eleanor Roosevelt, the famous reformer, humanitarian, and philanthropist.

He was the youngest of eight children and was of Cherokee descent. His father was a successful rancher and banker. His parents wanted him to be a minister, but he wanted to perform in a circus. He was well-coordinated, but careless in his personal hygiene. Although he excelled in history and social studies, he received poor grades in school, did not complete his work, and was expelled. His special skills included a sense of humor and recitation. His name was Will Rogers, the famous entertainer, orator, and nominee for President of the United States.

She came from a low-income family. She had two sisters; her mother was a domestic worker and her father was a minister. She was overweight, and later developed multiple sclerosis. Although a very quiet child, she possessed a sense of humor, was charismatic, eloquent, humble, and a leader. Ambitious and hardworking, her name was Barbara Jordan, the famous Congresswoman and orator.

He came from a middle class family of seven children. His father was a carpenter. He had an enlarged head at birth and was not able to talk until he was almost 4 years old. He was enrolled in school 2 years late due to scarlet fever and respiratory infections. He lost his hearing and had a high-pitched voice. His attendance in school was poor. He was stubborn, aloof, shy, self-centered, and disengaged with the learning process, and he did not seem to care about school. One teacher said that his brains were addled, even though he had an excellent memory, read well, displayed perseverance, asked questions, and was a good problem solver. He liked to build things and wanted to earn money. His name was Thomas Edison, the famous inventor.

Born to an undistinguished family, he moved often with his father, sister, and brother. His mother died when he was small and his father, a farmer, remarried. He was once kicked in the head by a horse and thought dead. He had Marfan syndrome, a genetic disease that affects connective tissues, including those around the heart, skeleton, and nervous system. He briefly attended school and was considered lazy. He excelled at sports, was an avid reader, and liked practical jokes. He was a good debater and thinker and also liked to argue. Interested in sales, he wanted to open his own business. His name was Abraham Lincoln, the former President of the United States.

She was a fatherless child whose mother struggled financially. Suffering from dyslexia, she could not read, write, or do mathematical problems. Teachers described her as a class clown. She left school at age 16. Her name is Cherilyn Sarkisian LaPiere—Cher—the famous entertainer.

His teachers viewed him as bright, but inattentive and lazy. He was viewed by some of his classmates as crazy or "retarded." Each day, in elementary school, as his turn to read aloud approached, he went to the bathroom, where he got sick to his stomach and wished he would die. Unfortunately, when he returned to the room, it was always still his turn to read aloud. In sixth grade, when assigned a composition, he dictated an outstanding composition to his mother, because his poor handwriting and spelling interfered with his work production. He was accused of plagiarism, and became so disconsolate he dropped out of school for a time. In college, the student met with each of his professors prior to each semester. He described to them his love of literature and his passion for writing. He also described his needs to take periodic breaks during class due to his Attention Deficit/Hyperactivity Disorder (ADHD), to receive copies of a peer's notes, to do all major writing on the word processor due to his written language disability, and to have books on tape because he read on a seventh-grade level. The professors invariably agreed to work closely with him. Jonathan Mooney graduated from Brown University with honors and a 4.0 average. Now an inspirational speaker and author, he shares his experiences and the positive impact of appropriate adaptations and accommodations in his book, *Learning Outside the Lines* (Mooney & Cole, 2000).

Her previous teacher advised Mary's new teacher that her writing was terrible. It contained little or no punctuation, run on sentences, and few capital letters. But the new teacher took the time to actually read her writing. He was struck by the creativity it revealed. He pulled Mary aside and told her to keep on writing and not to worry about the mechanics, but just focus on her wonderful ideas. Today, at 40 years old, Mary is a special education teacher with a master's degree in education. She graduated magna cum laude from college with a degree in philosophy and literature; became an attorney working in criminal defense, civil rights, and legal assistance for those with mental illness; and returned to the classroom as an educator to support middle school students with challenges. The child, Mary White, whose teacher said that she could not write received the Hart Crane Memorial Award for her poetry (Hardy, 2010).

These are profiles of people who were smart and overcame their learning difficulties. Think about all of our kids sitting in classrooms today who are smart, but struggle in school. Their school experiences may mirror those profiled above. Unfortunately, they may not have the resilience to succeed despite their circumstances.

Imagine the impact if all of these kids were given the tools that could ease their struggle and the contributions they could make if they were given strategies to succeed.

POPULATION

So who are these students and what characteristics can we look for to identify them? Bright students who are not reaching their potential present themselves in different ways, depending on what is contributing to their lack of achievement. Sometimes their difficulty in school is due to a documented learning disability. Sometimes it may be due to a health impairment such as ADHD. At other times, they may be students with neurological differences, such as autism spectrum disorder, that provide challenges to their learning. In addition to the more typical learning disabilities like spelling and writing difficulties, organization, word retrieval, and processing speed, some students struggle with nonverbal learning disabilities, those characterized by problems in visual-spatial, organizational, tactile-perceptual, and psychomotor skills (see Table 1) that adversely affect their academic performance with rigorous instruction.

Despite their outstanding abilities, smart students with learning difficulties often have problems with the physical production of schoolwork, and with the written output, organization, memory, and reading school requires. At other times, these kids seem to be average students because their brightness

Table1

Definitions Related to Nonverbal Learning Disabilities

Term	Definition
visual-spatial	learning by seeing (e.g., diagrams, maps, graphs, facial expressions, and body language)
organization	bringing order to self, place, and materials
tactile-perceptual	learning through sensory input
psychomotor	muscular activity directly related to mental processes

and their learning difficulties are masking one another. There are also students who, despite a lack of any documented disability, are underachieving or not performing to their potential. These students are often the most difficult to understand and reach because they do not fall into a neat category with specific instructional skills that can be addressed. Understanding who these students are, the struggles they face, how to best address their needs, and the roles parents and educators play in their lives is essential if smart kids with learning problems are to develop intellectually, socially, and emotionally.

As you become actively involved in helping your child succeed, it is important for you to have a common understanding of the definitions and terms used in both the field of gifted education and the realm of special education. The following definitions will help facilitate communication between yourself and school personnel and clarify what groups of students we are referring to in this book. This knowledge will contribute to your effectiveness and efficiency in advocating for appropriate programming and identification decisions for your child.

Definition of Gifted and Talented Students

The National Association for Gifted Children (NAGC, 2008a) defined gifted and talented students in its position statement, "Redefining Giftedness for a New Century: Shifting the Paradigm" as:

Gifted individuals are those who demonstrate outstanding levels of aptitude (defined as an exceptional ability to reason and learn) or competence (documented performance or achievement in top 10% or rarer) in one or more domains. Domains include any structured area of activity with its own symbol system (e.g., mathematics, music, language) and/or set of sensorimotor skills (e.g., painting, dance, sports).

The development of ability or talent is a lifelong process. It can be evident in young children as exceptional performance on tests and/or other measures of ability or as a rapid rate of learning, compared to other students of the same age, or in actual achievement in a domain. As individuals mature through childhood to adolescence, however, achievement and high levels of motivation in the domain become the primary characteristics of their giftedness. Various factors can either enhance or inhibit the development and expression of abilities. (para. 4–5)

Federal education policy, the No Child Left Behind Act (NCLB, 2001), defines gifted and talented students as

students, children, or youth who give evidence of high achievement capability in areas such as intellectual, creative, artistic, or leadership capacity, or in specific academic fields, and who need services or activities not ordinarily provided by the school in order to fully develop those capabilities. (p. 544)

In addition, the Jacob K. Javits Gifted and Talented Students Education Act (1988) provides us with another good definition of gifted and talented students as:

Those children and youth with outstanding talent [who] perform or show the potential for performing at remarkably high levels of accomplishment when compared with others of their age, experience, or environment. These outstanding talents are present in children and youth from all cultural groups, across all economic strata, and in all areas of human endeavor. (Title IV, Sec. 4101)

Definition of Learning Disabilities

The Individuals with Disabilities Education Act (IDEA) was first signed into law in 1975. It was later updated in 2004. This legislation provides a good definition of learning disabilities as defined by federal law.

In general, the term *specific learning disability* indicates a disorder in one or more of the basic psychological processes involved in understanding or in using language. This includes spoken or written language. In addition, federal law notes that the disability may manifest itself in the imperfect ability to listen, think, speak, read, write, spell, or do mathematical calculations (IDEA, 2004).

Disorders considered to be learning disabilities include conditions such as perceptual disabilities, brain injuries, minimal brain dysfunction, dyslexia, and developmental aphasia (a language impairment caused by brain damage). However, federal law does not include learning problems that are primarily the result of visual, hearing, or motor disabilities; of mental retardation; of emotional disturbance; or of environmental, cultural, or economic disadvantages (IDEA, 2004).

The DSM 5, the fifth edition of the American Psychiatric Association's (2013a) *Diagnostic and Statistical Manual of Mental Disorders* (DSM-5), includes criteria for diagnosing learning disorders. The DSM-5 is the standard reference system used by mental health professionals and physicians for diagnosis of disorders. Diagnoses inform school 504 and IEP teams and can lead to decisions about educational disabilities. The DSM 5 includes changes in diagnosing learning disorders that combines the DSM-IV (2000) diagnoses of reading disorder, mathematics disorder, disorder of written expression, and learning disorder not otherwise specified. The text also acknowledges that learning deficits are described internationally in various ways, including as dyslexia, dysgraphia, and dyscalculia (APA, 2013b) For more information about learning disorders, as described in the DSM 5, we encourage the reader to visit the DSM's website at http://www.dsm5.org or the Learning Disabilities Association of America's website at http://www.ldanatl.org

Definition of Gifted and Talented/ Learning Disabled Students

Those students who possess an outstanding gift or talent and are capable of high performance, but who also have a learning disability that makes some aspect of academic achievement difficult are considered to be gifted and talented and learning disabled (GT/LD). Often called *twice-exceptional*, these students meet the definitions for both gifted and talented and learning disabled students.

The use of the term *gifted and talented/learning disabled* has historical significance. It was the terminology used in Maryland's Montgomery County Public School system's first GT/LD program focusing on the strengths and needs of this population and also in other programs in the United States. Over the years, twice-exceptional has become the more frequently used term because it includes students with other disabilities beyond just learning disabilities. Although our preferred term is *smart kids with learning difficulties*, we will use all of these terms interchangeably. We believe strongly that *smart kids with learning difficulties* is more inclusive, understandable, and user-friendly, because not every student in this population has been identified as gifted and/or with a specific disability.

According to the National Education Association's (2006) position paper *The Twice-Exceptional Dilemma*, twice-exceptional students can be difficult to define because there is great variability within this population:

> The one common characteristic of this group, however, is that they simultaneously possess attributes of giftedness as well as learning, physical, social/emotional, or behavioral deficits. These students are found within every cultural, socioeconomic, racial, and ethnic group and may be gifted students with physical disabilities, sensory disabilities, Asperger's syndrome, emotional

and/or behavioral disorders, Attention-Deficit/Hyper-activity Disorder, and Learning Disabilities. (p. 5–6)

The following definition of 2E learners and their educational needs is a product of a symposium that we were involved in during the Summer of 2009 at the University of Connecticut with many of the national leaders in this field, including Dr. Sally Reis and Dr. Susan Baum. Twice-exceptional learners are students who evidence the potential for high achievement capability in areas such as specific academics, general intellectual ability, creativity, leadership, and/or visual, spatial, or performing arts, and also evidence one or more disabilities as defined by federal or state eligibility criteria, such as specific learning disabilities, speech and language disorders, emotional/behavioral disorders, physical disabilities, autism spectrum disorders, or other health impairments, such as ADHD. Identification of twice-exceptional students requires comprehensive assessment in both the areas of giftedness and disability, as one does not preclude the other.

Educational services must address both the high achievement potential and the deficits of this population of students. Twice-exceptional students require differentiated instruction, accommodations, direct services, specialized instruction, acceleration options, and opportunities for talent development. Most twice-exceptional students require a 504 plan with accommodations or an Individualized Education Plan (IEP) with goals, accommodations, and strategies that enable them to achieve growth at a level commensurate with their abilities, develop their gifts and talents, and learn compensation skills and strategies to address their disabilities.

Definitions, services, and programs for twice-exceptional students differ from state to state. For example, in *Twice-Exceptional: Students With Both Gifts and Challenges or Disabilities* by the Idaho State Department of Education (2010), twice-exceptional is defined as:

Students who are identified as gifted and talented in one or more areas of exceptionality (specific academics, intellectual ability, creativity, leadership, visual or performing arts) and also identified with one or more specific diagnosable conditions [which may not be diagnosed], such as learning disabilities, mental health problems, neurological disorders, physical handicaps, or the asynchronicity that occurs due to the discrepancy between mental age and chronological age that may or may not impede their progress in life. (p. 1)

In the Colorado State Department of Education's (2009) *Twice-Exceptional Students: Gifted Students With Disabilities* (2nd ed.), the definition for gifted includes twice-exceptional students:

Gifted children means those persons between the ages of five and twenty-one whose abilities, talents, and potential for accomplishment are so exceptional or developmentally advanced that they require special provisions to meet their educational programming needs. Gifted and talented children are hereafter referred to as gifted students. Children under five who are gifted may also be provided with early childhood special educational services. Gifted students include gifted students with disabilities (i.e., twice-exceptional) and students with exceptional abilities or potential from all socio-economic and ethnic, cultural populations. Gifted students are capable of high performance, exceptional production, or exceptional learning behavior by virtue of any or a combination of these areas of giftedness:
- General or specific intellectual ability,
- Specific academic aptitude,
- Creative or productive thinking,
- Leadership abilities,
- Visual arts, performing arts, musical or psychomotor abilities. (p. 17)

The Wrightslaw website (see http://www.wrightslaw.com/info/2e.index.htm) offers an interactive map to find each state's policies on twice-exceptional children.

Definition of Gifted and Talented/ADHD Students

Some students possess an outstanding gift or talent and are capable of high performance, but also have been identified as having ADHD.

The DSM-5 (APA, 2013a) classifies ADHD as falling into two symptom domains, inattention and hyperactivity/impulsivity. Students must have "several" symptoms from both school (or work) and from home to qualify. The latest age of onset of symptoms has been changed to 12 years old in the DSM 5. It was previously 7 in the DSM-IV. Students with autism spectrum disorders may also qualify as having an additional and separate diagnosis of ADHD (APA, 2013b) For more information about ADHD, as described in the DSM 5, we encourage the reader to visit the DSM's website at http://www.dsm5.org or the Children and Adults with Attention-Deficit Hyperactivity Disorder (CHADD) website at http://www.chadd.org.

Diagnosis of ADHD in gifted students can be very difficult, and should only be done by a trained professional. Some of the characteristics used to identify students who have ADHD are also characteristics of gifted students in general, gifted students who have other disabilities (including learning disabilities), and bright underachieving students. However, many gifted students, with or without other disabilities, are also impacted by ADHD. Appropriate diagnosis by a mental health professional or doctor is crucial. The identification criteria described above require that some symptoms be present before age 7, and that some impairment is present in two or more settings; this will certainly help define the existence of ADHD as a disorder separate from the child's gifts or other learning difficulties.

Our experience has shown that some students who appear to have ADHD will no longer demonstrate the same symptoms, or the same symptoms to the extent that they would be considered a disability, when they are given an appropriate educational environment. On the other hand, it has been our experience that some students will continue to demonstrate symptoms of ADHD even when the best practices of working with twice-exceptional students are in place. These students may need both medical intervention and behavioral strategies that directly address these attention issues. Keep in mind that all diagnoses and any medical interventions should only be made by a trained psychiatrist, medical doctor, or other mental health professional.

Colleen Willard-Holt (1999) identified the following questions to ask when you think that your child may be showing signs of having ADHD:

- Could the behaviors be responses to inappropriate placement, insufficient challenge, or lack of intellectual peers?
- Is the child able to concentrate when he is interested in the activity?
- Have any curricular modifications been made in an attempt to change his inappropriate behaviors?
- Has the child been interviewed? What are his or her feelings about the behaviors?
- Does the child feel out of control? Do the parents perceive the child as being out of control?
- Do the behaviors occur at certain times of the day, during certain activities, with certain teachers, or in certain environments? (¶ 12)

Answering these questions will help you begin the process of determining if a disability such as ADHD may exist in the smart kids you know.

Definition of Gifted Students With Autism

Gifted students with autism (including those who had previously been diagnosed with Asperger's syndrome, high-functioning autism, or Nonverbal Learning Disorder) are students who possess an outstanding gift or talent and are capable of high performance and also have autism spectrum disorder.

An autism spectrum disorder (ASD) includes the previously named autistic disorders of Asperger's syndrome, high-functioning autism, Nonverbal Learning Disorder, Childhood Disintegrative Disorder, and Pervasive Developmental Disorder–Not Otherwise Specified.

ASD is characterized by:

- deficits in social communication and social interaction; and
- restricted repetitive behaviors, interests, and activities.

There is a newly named disorder included in the DSM 5, called Social Communication Disorder, which will be the better fit for some of the students previously diagnosed with Asperger's syndrome, Nonverbal Learning Disorder, or Pervasive Developmental Disorder–Not Otherwise Specified.

A person will meet the criteria for Social Communication Disorder, if she meets all of the criteria for autism spectrum disorder, except for Part B (restrictive, repetitive patterns of behavior, interests, or activities; APA, 2013b). For more information about ASD, as described in the DSM 5, we encourage the reader to visit the DSM's website at http://www.dsm5.org or the Autism Speaks website at http://www.autismspeaks.org.

It seems clear that schools will determine that most students who meet the criteria for autism spectrum disorder and who have both educational impact and the need for specialized instruction will qualify for the educational disability of autism. It also seems likely that students who qualify for the new category of Social Communication Disorder and who have both educational impact and the need for specialized instruction will be found to be eligible for services under the category of Speech and Language Impairment.

It is important for you and your child to understand his or her own strengths and weaknesses. Gifted students with autism spectrum disorders and social communication disorders generally have difficulties in the following areas:

- communication,
- social skills,
- range of interests,
- sensory integration, and
- behavior.

On the other hand, students with autism spectrum disorders and social communication disorders may demonstrate great strengths, including:

- advanced reading of words (but not necessarily the same level of comprehension),
- fund of information,
- ability to memorize lists and facts,
- passion for learning,
- desire to share knowledge, and
- advanced vocabulary.

In summary, most gifted students who had previously been identified as having Asperger's syndrome, high-functioning autism, or Nonverbal Learning Disorder, will now be identified as either having autism spectrum disorders or Social Communication Disorder. We urge you to consult professionals when seeking this kind of diagnosis for your child.

Definition of Bright Underachieving Students

Many kids are smart and underachieving and could benefit from the same interventions that should be given to GT/LD kids, but they may not be identified as either gifted and talented or learning disabled. All of the strategies discussed later in this book can be used to help bright, underachieving students succeed in school.

Researchers have described the following three general themes when classifying gifted, underachieving students (Reis & McCoach, 2000):
- a discrepancy between potential (or ability) and performance (or achievement),
- a discrepancy between predicted achievement and actual achievement, and
- a failure to develop or utilize latent potential without reference to external criteria and without defining or measuring potential.

Like GT/LD students, bright, underachieving students typically demonstrate outstanding abilities in either the verbal or visual-spatial area. Despite these outstanding abilities, they typically have problems producing or completing schoolwork, particularly in the area of written output. Organization, memory, and reading also may be significantly impacted. There may be a discrepancy between what the student is able to conceptualize and what he actually produces.

When addressing underachievement, Drs. Fernette Eide and Brock Eide (n.d.) have suggested that there are various factors that need to be weighed for twice-exceptional students. These include: perfectionism and reverse perfectionism, test-taking ability, learning and processing styles, hidden agendas, poor self-concept, immaturity, focused interests, and emotional, philosophical, and physiological restlessness. Twice-exceptional advocate and researcher Linda Neumann (2010) noted that twice-exceptional students don't choose to underachieve and discussed the many factors that impact work output. There are the weaknesses and issues related to learning disabilities as well as factors like stress, competition, flexibility, and adaptability.

The term *underachieving* has a negative connotation that does not fit some of these students. A student with a documented learning disability who is also gifted and talented may take exception to being labeled as underachieving, especially in cases when it is her disability that is impacting her level of productivity, not a lack of motivation.

There are many articles and books related to underachievement in gifted and GT/LD kids. An excellent resource for articles can be found on the Davidson Institute for Talent Development website (http://www.davidsongifted.org)

CHARACTERISTICS

Students with gifts who also have learning challenges that affect their performance are often misunderstood and sometimes regarded as lazy or apathetic. Although the characteristics of these students vary greatly from student to student, there are some general commonalities.

These kids are in every classroom. They may look like other kids in the class, appearing to be average learners, as their strengths and weaknesses cancel out one another, or these kids may stand out because of their poor behavior, lack of achievement, or disorganization. Smart kids with learning difficulties can be highly verbal, expressing great insights and knowledge, yet they may never complete their written work. Or these students may contribute very little verbal expression to the class, yet they excel in hands-on activities. They may be reading below grade level and unable to remember simple directions. They may be holding it together in school, but falling apart at home. Smart students with learning challenges are likely to be experiencing problems related to some or all of the stumbling blocks that are described in detail later in this book.

Table 2 presents characteristics that may look very familiar to you; it provides a list of many of the characteristics found in smart kids who struggle in school due to learning problems. You can use it to help you understand your child or student better.

Table 2

Comparison of Characteristics of Gifted Students With or Without Disabilities

Characteristics of Gifted Students Without Disabilities	Characteristics of Gifted Students With Disabilities
Ability to learn basic skills quickly and easily and retain information with less repetition	Often struggle to learn basic skills due to cognitive processing difficulties; need to learn compensatory strategies in order to acquire basic skills and information
High verbal ability	High verbal ability, but extreme difficulty in written language area; may use language in inappropriate ways and at inappropriate times
Early reading ability	Frequently have reading problems due to cognitive processing deficits
Keen powers of observation	Strong observation skills, but often have deficits in memory skills
Strong critical thinking, problem-solving, and decision-making skills	Excel in solving real-world problems; outstanding critical thinking and decision-making skills; often independently develop compensatory skills
Long attention span— persistent, intense concentration	Frequently have attention deficit problems, but may concentrate for long periods in areas of interest
Questioning attitude	Strong questioning attitudes; may appear disrespectful when questioning information, facts, etc. presented by teacher
Creative in the generation of thoughts, ideas, actions; innovative	Unusual imagination; frequently generate original and, at times, rather bizarre ideas; extremely divergent in thought; may appear to daydream when generating ideas
Take risks	Often unwilling to take risks with regard to academics; take risks in nonschool areas without consideration of consequences
Unusual, often highly developed sense of humor	Humor may be used to divert attention from school failure; may use humor to make fun of peers or to avoid trouble
May mature faster at different rates than age peers	Sometimes appears immature because they may use anger, crying, withdrawal, etc. to express feelings and to deal with difficulties
Sense of independence	Require frequent teacher support and feedback in deficit areas; highly independent in other areas; often appear to be extremely stubborn and inflexible

Table 2, *continued*

Characteristics of Gifted Students Without Disabilities	Characteristics of Gifted Students With Disabilities
Sensitive	Sensitive regarding disability area(s); highly critical of self and others including teachers; can express concern about the feelings of others even while engaging in antisocial behavior
May not be accepted by other children and may feel isolated	May not be accepted by other children and may feel isolated; may be perceived as loners, because they do not fit typical model for either a gifted or a learning disabled student; sometimes have difficulty being accepted by peers due to poor social skills
Exhibit leadership ability	Exhibit leadership ability; often leader among the more nontraditional students; demonstrate strong streetwise behavior; the disability may interfere with ability to exercise leadership skills
Wide range of interests	Wide range of interests, but are handicapped in pursuing them due to process/learning problems
Very focused interests (i.e., a passion about certain topics to the exclusion of others)	Very focused interests (i.e., a passion about a certain topic to the exclusion of others) often not related to school subjects

Note. From *Comparison of Characteristics of Gifted Students With or Without Disabilities*, by D. Higgins, L. Baldwin, & D. Pereles, 2000, Unpublished manuscript. Reprinted with permission of the authors.

- Bright students who are not reaching their potential present themselves in different ways, depending on what is contributing to their lack of achievement.
- The characteristics of students with gifts who also have learning challenges that affect their performance vary greatly from student to student.
- Some general commonalities of GT/LD (twice-exceptional) kids are that they:
  o struggle to learn basic skills due to processing difficulties;
  o exhibit high verbal ability, but difficulty writing;
  o exhibit reading problems due to cognitive processing deficits;
  o exhibit strong observation skills, but deficits in memory;
  o excel in solving real-world problems, critical thinking, and decision-making;
  o exhibit attention problems, but may concentrate for long periods of time in areas of interest;
  o exhibit strong questioning attitudes;
  o possess imagination;
  o exhibit divergent thinking
  o take risks in nonschool areas, but are unwilling to take risks with regard to academics;
  o exhibit a keen sense of humor;
  o appear immature;
  o require frequent teacher support and feedback in deficit areas, yet are highly independent in other areas;
  o exhibit sensitivity and are highly critical of self and others;
  o may feel isolated and have difficulty with peers;
  o exhibit leadership qualities; and
  o enjoy a wide range of interests.

TIPS AND TOOLS

Supplementary materials included in this section:

- ➢ They Did It! So Can I!

- ➢ Characteristics of Gifted Students With Disabilities Checklist

They Did It! So Can I!

Some well-known individuals can provide inspiration for smart kids with learning disabilities, their parents, and their teachers. It helps to understand that others who we look to as successful role models have also experienced learning difficulties.

TIPS

Teacher

Use with the whole class, small groups, or individual students in conjunction with a research unit integrated into the curriculum. For example, if a character in a literary piece has learning challenges, this activity will give students insight to challenges others have faced. You can help your students recognize that kids with learning challenges have great potential for success.

Parent

Use with your child to heighten awareness that people do overcome challenges. Read about the lives of famous people with learning difficulties as a family and discuss their struggles, strategies, and successes.

Student

Learn about others who have been able to overcome their personal obstacles. Think about how their stories relate to you. Remember, it is OK to be different.

They Did It!

The famous people on this list have all faced learning difficulties in their lives and have overcome those difficulties to be successful adults. Using this list and the directions that follow, research a famous person who has overcome his or her learning problems to become successful.

Hans Christian Andersen	Henry Ford	Michael Phelps
Stephen Bacque	James Franco	Pete Rose
Ann Bancroft (explorer)	Danny Glover	Nolan Ryan
Harry Belafonte	Whoopi Goldberg	Charles Schwab
Alexander Graham Bell	Salma Hayek	Steven Spielberg
Mayim Bialik	Tommy Hilfiger	Jackie Stewart
Orlando Bloom	Bruce Jenner	Quentin Tarantino
Erin Brockovich	Jewel	Sting
Tim Burton	Magic Johnson	Diane Swonk
Stephen J. Cannell	Keira Knightley	Helen Taussig
James Carville	John Lennon	Bella Thorne
Winston Churchill	Jay Leno	Justin Timberlake
Anderson Cooper	David Letterman	Lindsay Wagner
Bill Cosby	Adam Levine	Henry Winkler
Tom Cruise	Carl Lewis	Robin Williams
Leonardo Da Vinci	Greg Louganis	Woodrow Wilson
Walt Disney	Edward James Olmos	Ahmet Zappa
Malcolm Forbes	Ty Pennington	

Directions:
1. Choose a person from the list above or from another source.
2. Research information about the person.
3. Once you have collected information, create a product that informs an audience about the individual you have studied. You may:
    a. write a blog,
    b. make a storyboard,
    c. design an exhibit,
    d. make a scrapbook,
    e. design a website,
    f. record information,
    g. create a video,
    h. perform a skit,
    i. create a podcast,
    j. create a PowerPoint presentation,
    k. create a collage, or
    l. design your own product.

Characteristics of Gifted Students With Disabilities Checklist

The following page provides a checklist of characteristics of students who are gifted, but also face learning challenges. It can be used to help identify these students.

TIPS

Teacher

Study the characteristics checklist. Observe your students. Create a list of students in your class who exhibit these characteristics. Use the information to help identify these students; provide interventions, programs, and services; and conference with parents.

Parent

Study the characteristics checklist. Observe your child. Share your observations and questions with your child's teacher and other staff members. Talk with your child about these characteristics and his or her strengths and weaknesses.

Student

Talk to your parents and teachers about your strengths, interests, and needs, and how they relate to the characteristics that describe you.

Characteristics of Gifted Students With Disabilities Checklist

❑ Often struggle to learn basic skills due to cognitive processing difficulties; need to learn compensatory strategies in order to acquire basic skills and information

❑ High verbal ability, but extreme difficulty in written language area; may use language in inappropriate ways and at inappropriate times

❑ Frequently have reading problems due to cognitive processing deficits

❑ Strong observation skills, but often have deficits in memory skills

❑ Excel in solving real-world problems; outstanding critical thinking and decision-making skills; often independently develop compensatory skills

❑ Frequently have attention deficit problems, but may concentrate for long periods in areas of interest

❑ Strong questioning attitudes; may appear disrespectful when questioning information, facts, etc. presented by teacher

❑ Unusual imagination; frequently generate original and at times rather bizarre ideas; extremely divergent in thought; may appear to daydream when generating ideas

❑ Often unwilling to take risks with regard to academics; take risks in nonschool areas without consideration of consequences

❑ Humor may be used to divert attention from school failure; may use humor to make fun of peers or to avoid trouble

❑ Sometimes appear immature because they may use anger, crying, or withdrawal to express feelings and to deal with difficulties

❑ Require frequent teacher support and feedback in deficit areas; highly independent in other areas; often appear to be extremely stubborn and inflexible

❑ Sensitive regarding disability area(s); highly critical of self and others, including teachers; can express concern about the feelings of others even while engaging in antisocial behavior

❑ May not be accepted by other children and may feel isolated; may be perceived as loners, because they do not fit the typical model for either a gifted or a learning-disabled student; sometimes have difficulty being accepted by peers due to poor social skills

❑ Exhibit leadership ability; often the leader among the more nontraditional students; demonstrate strong streetwise behavior;

sometimes the disability may interfere with the ability to exercise leadership skills

❑ Wide range of interests but are handicapped in pursuing them due to processing/learning problems

❑ Very focused interest (i.e., a passion about a certain topic to the exclusion of others) often not related to school subjects

2

How Do We Identify Smart Kids With Learning Difficulties?

Identification

Students who are bright and have learning challenges need to be carefully identified so that they can receive both the challenge and support they need and deserve. Successful identification consists of many pieces. The pieces may not make sense in isolation, but together they can eventually provide a clear understanding of an individual child's educational history, strengths, needs, and learning styles. The first step is to help those holding the individual pieces—the student, parents, teachers, and school—to recognize them and figure out how they fit together.

As a parent, you, of course, are your child's first teacher and you bear the ultimate responsibility for making educational choices. You are probably concerned about the

 DOI:10.4324/9781003237983-3

average (or below average) performance of your child, who you know is bright, but you may not be aware of the resources that are available to you. You may not even be aware of your right to request an educational evaluation if you suspect that your child may have an educational disability that requires the provision of special education and related services. As a result, your pieces may be the last to fall into place. However, if in using the materials in this book you suspect that your child may have disabilities that need to be addressed by his school, a phone call to his teacher or counselor can initiate the identification process and open up discussion of your child's needs. Parents and teachers must work collaboratively to develop appropriate educational services for all children.

In identifying the twice-exceptional learner, best practices call for a comprehensive evaluation that includes as much information as possible about the student's cognitive and academic abilities, as well as her social-emotional profile, in order that the appropriate learning environment be provided in which the student's strengths are recognized and given attention while her areas of need are simultaneously addressed.

Regardless of the circumstances, smart students with learning challenges have repeatedly reported that school is a difficult and frustrating experience. Some student's behaviors (whether acting out or shutting down) do provide clues to their parents that the formal identification process for diagnosis as gifted and talented or for having learning disabilities should be considered. At other times, it is the teachers who are sensitive to and address these students' apparent school performance difficulties carefully and proactively through school meetings that get the ball rolling with the identification process. The importance of early identification and intervention has been well-documented. The earlier we find the kids who need additional services and the earlier we provide appropriate programming for these kids, the more successful the interventions will be.

If you are a teacher, you should have the experience and training to identify students who are having learning problems. Guiding a student and his or her family through the identification process takes time, and you must work closely with the student's parents. Collaboration is critical to begin any special testing or other intervention. The identification process is crucial to an effective delivery of services for your smart students with learning problems.

Parents and teachers, remember that students themselves are critically important members of the team. These children are a puzzle even to themselves and are often greatly relieved when their learning difficulties are diagnosed and accommodated for because they no longer carry the burden of fault for their lack of success in school.

Parents, teachers, and students each need to understand their position of importance in the identification process. Delivery of appropriate educational services for bright students with learning difficulties is dependent on the quality of the working relationship between these students, their parents, and their teachers.

Gifted Identification

The National Association for Gifted Children (NAGC) is the preeminent organization in the nation to support the education of gifted children. In NAGC's October 2008 position paper on the role of assessments in the identification of gifted students, the organization stated that the process for identifying students for gifted and talented programs must have: (a) defensible measurement practices that are aligned with program goals and objectives, (b) administration and interpretation of assessments by properly trained persons, and (c) ethical decision making in program placement.

The NAGC (2008b) position paper also stated that assessments must be appropriate for and sensitive to students who have been traditionally underrepresented in gifted programs. The position paper supports the use of multiple criteria in the identification of gifted students, as well as participation of multiple stakeholders, including teachers, parents, and other gifted advocates in decision making, including never basing decisions on a single assessment.

To answer the question of how we can identify gifted learners in ways that are equitable and effective, a literature review highlighted the following points. Although multiple criteria continue to be important, only assessments that provide sound psychometric information on students regardless of language, culture, gender, race, or socioeconomic status should be used (VanTassel-Baska, 2007). This will ensure a more fair identification process. In addition, this identification process should be periodically reviewed to make sure that it is valid for the population being served and the types of services being provided (Coleman, 2003; National Education Association, 2006).

Many school districts conduct a broad-based gifted screening process for their students during the elementary years, usually between grades 2 and 5. To ensure that all students receive a fair opportunity to be identified, it is important that all students be screened and that no one is excluded from this process because of a disability.

There are some important principles that should be in place to ensure the screening procedures are accurate and thorough. First, schools should choose a committee that represents classroom teachers, special educators, art or music teachers, and others, including guidance counselors and media specialists. These varied perspectives and lenses are essential to compiling a complete picture of each student.

Second, keep in mind that effective screening and selection procedures use multiple criteria. Parents, teachers, and other school staff should be part of the process, and tests should include those that measure critical thinking, problem solving, and verbal and nonverbal reasoning. Recommendations from different persons and student work samples are good sources of information. Some of the best information may come from nontraditional sources, like portfolios and community nominations. It is important not to rely on only the test data and not to exclude a student because of one low indicator. We should not adhere to rigid cutoffs when evaluating performance on test data, but rather look at ranges of scores in relationship to all of the other data. A complete list of tools that can be used in identifying gifted students is included in the supplementary materials at the end of this chapter.

We must ensure that children from different backgrounds and experiences, including those with special needs and learning difficulties have a fair chance to be considered for gifted programs. Historically, gifted programs have not adequately identified and served African American and Hispanic students. In addition, girls typically have been underrepresented in rigorous math and science instruction. Today, we see an increasing trend of boys not being identified and not participating in rigorous instruction. Boys, especially minorities, continue to be disproportionately identified for special education. Advocacy on the part of staff, parents, or students must be a vital part of the process. Personal knowledge of students' strengths and interests may be more indicative of their abilities and potential than any objective assessment.

Schools that implement these principles will uphold the integrity of the screening process. However, school personnel must be ever mindful that they must continually assess children, for they grow and mature at different rates through their school years.

Parents, the school should communicate the specifics of the selection and decision-making processes to you in order to promote understanding and to build strong partnerships that will benefit your children. This communication should begin during your child's first years of schooling, for early recognition programs will foster and nurture the natural curiosity and creativity of children and serve as building blocks for future learning.

Gifted and Talented/Learning Disabled Identification

Why is identification important? Identification of smart kids with learning difficulties is important for both our society and for the individual. James Gallagher summed up the importance for our society in an often-cited quote from 1978, when he said,

> failure to help the gifted child reach his potential is a societal tragedy, the extent of which is difficult to measure but what is surely great. How can we measure the sonata unwritten, the curative drug undiscovered, the absences of political insight? They are the difference between what we are and what we could be as a society.

It may be easiest to understand the price that the individual student who is not identified may pay by looking at one smart kid with learning difficulties. Nathan was a third grader who was struggling with attention, reading, and writing. When given an IQ test he scored a 130, or the 98th percentile, in verbal comprehension and a 68, or the 1st percentile, in processing speed. Those hugely discrepant scores caught our attention and helped to describe a very bright student who was having great difficulties with any type of output. But what really made this case memorable was included in the background of the psycho-educational assessment. As the psychologist sought to connect with Nathan and understand him, she asked him to tell her his three wishes. Although other third-grade boys typically wished for a new gaming system, a million dollars, or an ATV vehicle, Nathan wished:

1. To have my teacher understand why I don't get my work done and to have her stop yelling at me as if I don't know anything.
2. Make sure that none of my friends have the kind of problems that I have.
3. That I will not get in trouble any more.

Nathan's three wishes showed the risk many of these students face: Students who are not identified as smart kids with learning difficulties are at risk for developing emotional problems, failing in school, and dropping out of school early. *The Twice-Exceptional Dilemma* (National Education Association, 2006) stated that it is crucial to recognize that unique learning needs must be met for students, that these students are a potential natural resource who will contribute to society, and that the whole child must be considered.

The process used to identify students as gifted with learning disabilities varies from one state to the next, as well as in school districts within a particular state. It is important to contact your state department of education, as well as your local school district, for the current guidelines for gifted identification. However, the process for identifying disabilities is governed by federal law. Guidance from the federal law changed in

2004 with implications that we will discuss later. The following is a discussion of some of the guidelines and practices used in a few states. Parents and teachers, we offer this discussion as a way to familiarize yourself with some of the guidelines already established by some school districts. However, you should contact your local school district and state department of education to get a full listing of their own guidelines and practices for identifying gifted students with learning disabilities.

Maryland is one of a few states to offer special guidelines for identifying GT/LD students. Colorado, Idaho, and Virginia have also published guidelines for identifying and working with twice-exceptional students. GT/LD students are often identified as learning disabled through special education procedures (Maryland State Department of Education [MSDE], 2000). Currently, when students are evaluated for a suspected learning disability, information becomes available about their strengths and challenges. The information revealed in IQ testing may serve to identify students as gifted who otherwise might have gone unidentified. Teachers are often surprised to discover that GTLD students can have a broad verbal or perceptual reasoning IQ score that is in the superior or very superior range, indicating evidence of superior abilities, especially when they have previously seen the daily struggle that a student is experiencing. At other times, a careful look at the subtests in the IQ testing shows significant gifts although, as a result of students' weaknesses averaging out their strengths, the broad verbal or performance scores look unremarkable.

Using the IQ and educational discrepancy range (a significant gap between achievement and aptitude) is one consideration among many when determining if a child qualifies as having a learning disability. (In our discussion of Response to Intervention [RtI], we will talk about other ways to determine this type of disability.) Maryland's (MSDE, 2001) learning disability identification guidelines include students who are functioning in the superior and very superior range. For example, a student who scores in a very superior range (130) on an intelligence test, but scores only average (100) on an education achievement test, would be said to have a significant discrepancy or difference. This difference is one indication that the student may have a learning disability. Many school districts have moved away from utilizing the discrepancy range, but still will look at patterns of strengths and weaknesses, as described in the federal law discussed further in The Law section.

In a letter to the Learning Disabilities Association of North Carolina, a representative of the United States Department of Education offered guidelines for the identification of GT/LD students, including:

- No child's IQ can be too high for that child to be considered for eligibility for special education services.
- Children can be considered for special education if they are not working at their ability level. To determine this, they must be given the opportunity to work at their ability level.
- We must take into consideration what the child's performance would be without the help and support of parents and outside providers like tutors and therapists (T. Hehir, personal communication to P. Lillie and R. Felton, April 5, 1995).

These guidelines have been reaffirmed in a Pennsylvania District Court case (West Chester Area School District v. Chad C., 2002), which stated that:

- students' grades that are declining (even if not failing) are not a reflection of their ability, and
- one must consider the child's potential when determining if he or she qualifies for service.

Notice that both the U.S. Department of Education's guidelines directed toward North Carolina's Learning Disabilities Association and those followed by the Maryland State Department of Education incorporate the use of IQ tests.

Although IQ tests are commonly used to help determine a child's giftedness, they are not and should not be the only method used to identify a student's strengths. Many school systems have developed and adopted additional ways to determine a child's giftedness.

Some GT/LD students have been and will continue to be identified by gifted screening processes. Keep in mind that for others the masking of their giftedness by their learning difficulties will leave them unidentified by general screening processes. It is crucial that the professionals who are identifying giftedness be familiar with characteristics of GT/LD students, as well as with the screening data for patterns that may suggest a gifted student with disabilities. Only an authorized school team can make the final determination that a child has a learning disability.

In addition to screening committees, Individualized Educational Program (IEP) teams must take special caution during the process of identifying gifted students with learning disabilities (MSDE, 2001). Consideration should be given to the unique profiles of GT/LD kids who present some strengths and, at first look, may not appear to need services.

Teams must recognize that a student may be gifted or have far-above-average ability and also have a specific learning disability. The specific learning disability may be manifested in an inability to complete class work at the level expected, given the student's high cognitive ability, without tutoring or support. Like students with learning disabilities, these gifted students may have organizational or processing weaknesses that make it difficult to achieve classroom expectations. For example, a student may have completed the homework, but cannot find it to hand in to the teacher or the student may turn in an outline rather than paragraphs because the student missed part of the directions.

In order to be identified with a specific learning disability, high-ability students should display evidence of a discrepancy between their cognitive ability and their achievement. For example, a student who is able to talk in detail about something, but can't write the same ideas on paper shows such a discrepancy. Although a discrepancy between ability and achievement should not be the only measure of a learning disability for high-ability students, it should be carefully considered as one indication that a disability exists (Brody & Mills, 1997).

These identification procedures can provide us with a guide to find GT/LD students. However, there are still inherent stumbling blocks to overcome in order to officially identify smart kids with learning disabilities as GT/LD in the schools.

Potential stumbling blocks to GT/LD identification.
First, there are students who are originally identified for their giftedness, while any learning disability they may have goes unnoticed because of their ability to compensate for their weaknesses. The disability or question of disability usually arises as the demand for written work increases in school. For example, in the primary grades (K–2), a student may appear bright because of his or her advanced vocabulary and oral expression, but when the writing demands increase, the student continues to use simple words and sentences.

Then, there are those students who are identified first by their learning disabilities; as a result, all of the attention given to them in school is directed at remediation. For example, students who are not able to read may be identified as needing special education services, leaving their teachers to never see evidence of their gifts. Inadequate assessments or depressed IQ scores often lead to an underestimation of their intellectual abilities. The result is that their areas of giftedness are not recognized or addressed. The severity of the learning disability is masking their giftedness. Only if and when a teacher or parent sees the spark of high ability in other areas is there a chance that these students' gifts are revealed.

And there are those students who may appear to be of average ability, because they are using all of their gifts to compensate for their areas of weakness. The giftedness and the learning disability are masking each other. These students are not getting services for either their gift or their disability.

Finally, there are those students who may have been identified as gifted, yet are exhibiting difficulties in school and are considered to be underachievers. They may be working at or near grade level. Their underachievement is often attributed to poor self-concept, lack of motivation, or laziness. Their superior gifts are masking their learning disability.

Regardless of the scenario, these students often carry with them a low self-concept because of the inner conflict they face—they know they are bright, but at the same time they are feeling frustrated by their shortcomings. Less easy to define, but equally important to identify, are students who are bright and experiencing learning challenges, but who do not qualify for the

GT, GT/LD, LD, or other label—the bright underachieving students. For a multimodal program that can be implemented to help underachieving students, see *School Success for Kids With ADHD* (Silverman, Iseman, & Jeweler, 2009).

Identification as GT With ADHD or GT With Autism Spectrum Disorders

The identification of a student as both gifted and having either ADHD or autism spectrum disorders requires cooperation between parents, psychologists and/or doctors, and educators. Information from intelligence tests, home performance checklists, and school performance checklists will provide evidence of the student's gifts. Behavioral checklists, expert analysis, and a combination of both objective and anecdotal evidence from the classroom will need to be compiled and carefully considered to determine if an educational disability is present.

RECOGNIZING AND FREEING POTENTIAL

Now that you've been given some background on the identification process, it's up to you as a parent to recognize the potential your child possesses. You probably already know your child is bright, but how do you work to unleash her potential and help her succeed despite her learning difficulties? The next section will help you pinpoint your child's potential for success in a few specific areas, ultimately aiding him in overcoming his obstacles and realizing his potential. In addition, the ORR charts presented in this section and in the supplementary materials at the end of this chapter can be given to your child's school when completed for consideration during the gifted or gifted/learning disabled screening processes.

The dictionary defines *potential* as "power; existing in possibility; capable of development into actuality." Potential may be an internal passion, it may be determined by circumstances and opportunities, or it may be a combination of all of these ideas.

Children give us clues that help us recognize their potential. As parents and teachers, we need to open our eyes to the everyday actions of our children. One process that can help kids find their power is called Observe and Reflect and Respond (ORR). ORR is a model for parents and educators to think about and act on children's behaviors. Observing and reflecting on behaviors in each of the following categories of characteristics can alert adults to the presence of potential. Once the behaviors are recognized, appropriate responses may help that potential become performance (Barnes-Robinson, Jeweler, & Ricci, 2004).

When observing and reflecting about children, it is helpful to begin by understanding what each of the following categories of characteristics mean in order to organize our thinking. The ORR charts in Figure 1 detail a child's actions in each of the following categories:

- *Thinking (cognitive)* is the process of logical thought. It is the act or process of knowing. Children often let us know what they are thinking about. They may tell us in words and/or show us through their actions and behaviors.
- *Responsibility (commitment)* occurs when a person is able to answer for his conduct or follow through on an agreement to do something. Children often show us through their actions and behaviors that they can start and finish a task or that they care deeply about something.
- *Breaking work into parts (task analysis)* is the ability to understand the steps to follow in order to complete an assigned piece of work. Your children may demonstrate that they understand how to successfully complete tasks.
- *Creative ability (imagination)* is when a person has a command of imagery and is able to be inventive. Children share their creations of the mind in a variety of ways, through the visual arts, music, literature, poetry, and architecture or engineering.
- *Appreciation of beauty (aesthetics)* is when an individual responds to beauty and the arts. Children can let us know verbally, nonverbally, and artistically that they recognize beautiful things.

- *Interactions with others (social)* can be defined as the co-operative and interdependent relationships of an individual with the members of a group. Children can be observed as they engage in activities with others and give insights into their interpersonal and intrapersonal selves (Barnes-Robinson et al., 2004).

The ORR charts in Figure 1 offer specific examples under each of the six categories. The first column describes a specific observable behavior you make about the child, the second column lists questions that you can ask yourself during reflection time, and the third column offers possible responses that may free the potential observed in the child. These are some examples designed as jumping off places for individualized responses.

What frees potential? Social, emotional, and sensory experiences shape the brain in the early years more than information. Our culture shapes us in the early years, too. That is when the brain has the most capacity to organize itself, taking advantage of all its neurons to lay the framework for language, music, math, and art. The cells do not engage in learning if there aren't opportunities, and without opportunities, the possible connections are never made (Barnes-Robinson et al., 2004).

A child's potential can be freed in different ways, including perceiving opportunities, recognizing requisite skills, and working in a positive climate. Potential is realized when there is motivation to work hard, and when there is an attainable goal in sight. It can be unlocked when there is someone who believes in you, someone who guides, supports, and expects you to succeed. Potential is realized where there is sheer will, and when there is faith in a future. It is unleashed when there is someone to nurture and develop a skill or talent in a child, even when there is little economic opportunity. And potential is recognized when a child sees someone she loves overcome the impossible to achieve something important.

Our role, as parents and teachers, is to offer guidance and direction to our children so they will explore their talents and realize their gifts. The ORR process can provide specific ideas that give inspiration, stimulation, and affirmation to children (Barnes-Robinson et al., 2004). Students who are gifted and

Observe	Reflect	Respond
Thinking (Cognitive)		
Sits alone and looks through reading materials for hours.	Does my child enjoy learning about things? What is my child interested in? Does my child understand what is read?	Ask questions about my child's reading materials. Collect books and articles that would interest my child. Provide a variety of reading materials to my child.
Asks questions about anything and everything.	What is my child curious about? How can I help my child answer questions?	Gather materials with my child to find answers to questions. Talk with my child about possible answers. Choose guiding questions to help my child answer question.
Finds connections and relationships between things.	What is the process my child uses to see connections?	Ask my child for observations of what is common or different between things. Ask my child to explain how the connections were made.
Remembers things that I forget.	Does my child have a strong memory?	Play memory games with my child. Memorize and recite poems and songs together.
Responsibility (Commitment)		
Brings home animals in need of care.	Does my child have an interest in animals? Does my child feel responsible for the animals?	Introduce my child to books about animals. Take my child to interview a veterinarian. Suggest helping a neighbor with a pet.
Tries hard even though mistakes are being made.	Does my child complete difficult tasks? Does my child deal well with frustration? Is my child persistent? Is my child a perfectionist?	Praise my child's efforts. Explain that a good way to learn is from our mistakes.
Finishes a project independently.	Is my child able to work alone? Do I help my child more than I need to?	Praise my child for completing tasks. Give my child added responsibilities at home.
Talks about helping people.	What opportunities could I offer my child to meet this need?	Join service organizations. Volunteer in the community. Discuss issues about fairness.
Is always ready for school on time.	Does my child take responsibility for himself?	Give my child additional opportunities for independence. Praise my child's organizational skills.

Figure 1. Completed ORR charts.

Observe	Reflect	Respond
Breaking Work Into Parts (Task Analysis)		
Explains how to play a complex game.	Is my child capable of doing more complicated tasks than I though possible?	Let my child explain the steps in a task to a younger sibling. Play complex games with my child. Ask my child to help me solve a problem.
Finishes long-term school projects with ease.	What time management skills does my child use?	Allow my child to become involved in extracurricular activities. Ask my child to help plan family activities.
Keeps a neat and organized bedroom.	Is this carried over to other aspects of my child's life?	Ask my child to help organize issues or needs around the house. Assist my child in transferring these skills to other areas when needed.
Recognizes different ways to solve the same problem.	Are my child's ideas more effective and efficient ways of solving a problem? Does my child see solutions in a different way?	Reinforce my child's unique thinking. Ask my child to explain the steps used to solve the problem.
Creative Ability (Imagination)		
Sits and plays make believe games.	Do my child's toys promote pretend play? Should I get involved during this play?	Acknowledge the value of the play. Get involved in the play. Introduce new scenarios to the play.
Draws pictures on the sidewalk, scraps of paper, and in the sand at the beach.	Does my child have an interest in drawing? How can I promote this interest?	Ask my child to draw something specific for me. Show examples of many kinds of drawing. Introduce different materials for drawing. Take my child to an art gallery.
Dances around the house to music in his or her head.	Does my child enjoy moving to a beat?	Clear a special space for my child to dance. Play a variety of music to move to. Ask if my child would like to take dance lessons.
Has fun playing with "any old stuff" around the house.	Is my child able to think about everyday objects in a different way?	Use questions to promote creative thinking about the items he plays with. Make suggestions: "Can you think of another use for this potato masher?"

Figure 1. Continued.

Observe	Reflect	Respond
Creative Ability (Imagination), continued		
Makes up stories about every day things.	How can I encourage this creativity without being judgemental? How do I nurture original thinking?	Encourage my child to be creative with stories. Ask questions that will force my child to give more details. Encourage my child to write stories down or dictate them to me.
Appreciation of Beauty (Aesthetics)		
Tells you about a beautiful sunset.	Does my child comment often about beauty in nature? Is my child observant?	Talk about colors, form, and composition in nature. Point out aesthetically pleasing things in the environment.
Recognizes beauty in art and architecture.	Does my child observe the environment for things of beauty?	Take my child to art galleries and museums. Take art books out of the public library for my child. Take a city architecture tour.
Is always listening to music.	What is it about the music my child appreciates? What kinds of music does my child listen to?	Take my child to a concert. Share my personal music library with my child.
Interactions With Others (Social)		
Sits by an aging relative and cuddles for a long time.	Does my child think about others' needs first?	Let my child know that the affection shown to the relative is important.
Has good friends.	What attributes does my child have that attracts good friends? Does my child prefer fewer good friends rather than many?	Create play dates for my child. Talk about the value of friendship. Read books about friendship.
Enjoys listening to and telling family stories.	Is my child family oriented? What will encourage my child's interest in family?	Arrange for family get-togethers. Write the family stories into a book.
Leads others.	What leadership qualities does my child have?	Allow my child to lead the family in an activity over the weekend. Enroll my child in leadership activities.

Note. From "Potential: Winged Possibilities to Dreams Realized!" by L. Barnes-Robinson, S. Jeweler, and M. C. Ricci, June 2004, *Parenting for High Potential*, pp. 20–25. Copyright ©2004 by National Association for Gifted Children. Reprinted with permission.

Figure 1. Continued.

simultaneously learning disabled certainly show evidence of a high achievement capability if those gathering the evidence know what to look for. It is crucial that those who are making the decisions about these capabilities understand how the disability may mask the gift and what these capabilities may, in fact, look like in students who are both gifted and learning disabled.

What inspires a child to want to try something new, practice a skill, and be persistent? A writer, athlete, inventor, artist, parent, or teacher may provide inspiration to our children. Other external sources of inspiration may include the drive for success, rewards, fame, and money. It is our response as parents and educators that can inspire a child to do better, try something new, learn from his mistakes, or help others.

Two other aspects of freeing potential are stimulation and affirmation. Many children need to be jumpstarted to begin a task or pursue an interest. A positive statement of encouragement from a peer, parent, or instructor can contribute to unleashing their potential. The reinforcement takes place through our words and our actions. This support acts as an affirmation for the child. Affirmation builds confidence, and confidence frees children to become risk takers (Barnes-Robinson et al., 2004).

THE LAW

Once your child's potential strengths have been noted, these can be considered in the gifted or GT/LD identification process. If your child has been identified as either gifted, GT/LD, or learning disabled, it's important for you to know your child's rights and his school's responsibilities under the law. This section will give you an overview of those legal rights and responsibilities, and hopefully provide you with the information you need to know to advocate for your child and the services she needs and deserves.

The concepts of gifted and talented and learning disabled are defined in federal and state laws. Although there is no specific legal mandate to serve those students who are GT/LD, a close look at the laws related to both giftedness and learning disabilities reveals language that can provide parents and staff with the support and guidance they need in order to effectively advocate for services. Several laws and policies refer to gifted students and students who are gifted with learning disabilities. A brief discussion of how the laws and policies may be interpreted to support the appropriate education of bright students with learning difficulties is also included below.

Gifted Students

Federal education policy defines gifted and talented students in terms of students who show evidence of their high achievement capability. Students who are gifted and simultaneously learning disabled certainly show evidence of a high achievement capability if those gathering the evidence know what to look for. It is crucial that those who are making the decisions about these capabilities understand how the disability may mask the gift and what these capabilities may, in fact, look like in students who are both gifted and learning disabled.

The federal and state governments monitor the annual yearly progress of students, according to a number of different measures. States would certainly benefit by identifying more GT/LD students as gifted and providing them with access to Advanced Placement and college preparatory programs. It will be crucial for states to help local school districts know how to identify these students and understand how to help these students succeed once they are placed in rigorous programs.

Many states had previously adopted some of the key concepts of the definition of gifted and talented students found in the Jacob K. Javits Act of 1988. The word *potential* in the Javits definition is very significant for GT/LD students, many of whose assessments and achievements provide evidence of their potential.

The services that are offered for gifted and talented students vary widely from state to state, with some states going as far as requiring an IEP for all gifted students, while other states have no mandate for gifted instruction. Several states have the same legal requirement (Child Find) for finding all gifted students who reside within their jurisdiction, whether they are in public or private schools. Parents and school personnel should check with their state department of education to see where their state stands in relation to gifted mandates and child find requirements.

Students With Learning Disabilities

There has been a major change in federal law regarding the method of determining whether a child has a specific learning disability. Schools are no longer required to take into consideration whether a child has a severe discrepancy between achievement and intellectual ability. Instead, schools may use a process that determines if the child responds to scientific, research-based interventions. This change may have a great impact on students who are GT/LD. It relieves school systems from the requirement to perform assessments in order to determine if a gifted student's school performance may be discrepant from the student's superior to very superior ability. On the other hand, school systems, although not required to do so, may still choose to do this type of testing and may also consider these discrepancies if they see evidence of a pattern of strengths and weakness that is indicative of a disability, in either their own assessments or a private assessment provided by the student's parents.

It is up to you, the parents, to show that your child does qualify for the specific learning disability designation when she is not responding to scientific, research-based interventions. More than ever, it will be crucial to document the interventions that are being used and the evidence of how your child is responding to the interventions over time. As a parent, you will want to ask for a specific timetable that describes when and how the effectiveness of the interventions will be measured, and you will need to know what the schools will be using for documentation. You may want to collect your own samples of your child's work over a period of time that will demonstrate whether or not she is acquiring the targeted skills. Curriculum-based assessments, district- and statewide testing, and traditional psychoeducational assessments can all still be a part of this documentation. Parents and educators of students who have demonstrated evidence of giftedness, but are performing at or below average in some or all of their academics should be aware that there may be a specific learning disability present.

Gifted and Learning Disabled

One promising part of the Individuals with Disabilities Education Act 2004 update is that gifted and talented students who are disabled is included in the groups of students whose needs have priority in the U.S. Department of Education grants to guide research, personnel preparation, and technical assistance. This is the first time that IDEA acknowledges the needs of twice-exceptional children. This opens the door for more attention and potentially more services to be provided for GT/LD students. States, local school districts, and universities will now be eligible to receive federal money to study and promote promising practices for these students. You will want to encourage your local and state school districts to be part of the research and staff development that will be available to benefit bright students with learning difficulties.

IEPs

There have been some promising developments in the interpretation of the federal law as it applies to the identification of students for specialized instruction and related services. One of the roadblocks to finding that twice-exceptional students qualify for an IEP is the assertion that school districts are only responsible for providing students with a basic floor of opportunity, not for developing potential. In contrast, Congress stated that one of the purposes of the special education law is that " . . . children with disabilities . . . be prepared to lead productive and independent adult lives, to the maximum extent possible" (IDEA, 2004, p. 3) Expanding on this concept, a Washington court ruled in 2006 (*J. L., M. L. and K. L. v. Mercer Island School District*) that specific methodologies need to be included in the IEP, and accommodations alone are not sufficient to meet this need. Rather than accommodations alone, specially designed instruction for improving the student's skills must be included in each IEP. IDEA includes the requirement that IEPs should be aimed at the outcomes of independence and self-sufficiency, which may open the door to more targeted and comprehensive services for twice-exceptional students (Weinfeld & Davis, 2008)

As described in *Special Needs Advocacy Resource Book* (Weinfeld & Davis, 2008), there is often disagreement between school and parents about whether an IEP should address areas other than academics, such as social skills and attendance. Schools sometimes take the view that when grades and test scores are at least at grade level, then there is no problem. Some twice-exceptional students, particularly those students with autism spectrum disorders or Social Communication Disorders, may not have academic deficiencies, yet they may display poor social or emotional skills. Parents who have challenged this have been successful, as in the case of *Mr. and Mrs. I. v. Maine School Administrative District 55* (2006), which concerned a child with Asperger's syndrome and social-emotional problems. The court's recommended decision recognized that educational performance encompasses more than merely academic performance. It then went on to state that "[w]hile a child's impairment need not necessarily manifest itself in academic failure, ... it must ... manifest itself in an adverse effect on the child's ability to learn" (p. 15). The IEP's contents and goals may span across a child's day and address attendance, social skills, executive functioning skills, coping skills, or adaptive skills (daily living skills) among others; the IEP content may not be limited to academic areas. As the new core curriculum is adopted throughout the United States, it identifies more of these learning skills as part of the curriculum. We believe that this will open the door to more gifted students with disabilities qualifying for IEPs, even if they are not deficient in reading, writing, or mathematics.

The identification of reading fluency as one of the areas of disability in IDEA should also open the door for more gifted students with disabilities qualifying for specialized instruction through an IEP. Many twice-exceptional students are able to learn the rules of decoding but do not read easily, quickly, or smoothly. As Dr. Alexa Posny, Acting Director of the Office of Special Education Programs wrote in a January 2010 letter, including reading fluency in IDEA 2004 makes it "more likely that a child who is gifted and has an SLD [specific learning disability] would be identified" (p. 2).

In the same letter, Dr. Posny specifically confirms the Department of Education's belief that "IDEA and its regulations do provide protections for high cognition and disabilities . . ." (p. 2). Dr. Posny gave weight to another important concept regarding eligibility for an IEP for twice-exceptional students in the 2010 letter mentioned above. She confirmed the Department of Education's

> long-standing position that, in general, it would be appropriate for the evaluation team to consider information about outside or extra learning support provided to the child to determine whether the child's current achievement reflects the service augmentation or what the child's achievement would be without such help. (p. 2)

Therefore, the IEP eligibility team must imagine what the child's academic performance would be without the tutoring, coaching, or therapies the parents may be providing.

In 2010, the U. S. District Court, Southern District of Texas issued an opinion with strong, positive repercussions for providing free appropriate public education (FAPE) for smart kids with learning difficulties. FAPE is a crucial concept of the federal laws involved with special education and accommodations. Under IDEA (2004), free appropriate public education means special education and related services that:

- are provided at public expense, under public supervision and direction;
- meet the standards of the Department of Education, including the requirements of IDEA;
- include preschool, elementary, or secondary education; and
- are provided in conformity with an IEP that meets the requirement of IDEA (pp. 7–8).

In the case of *Klein Independent School District and Texas Education Agency v. Per Hovem, Knut Hovem and Signe Hovem*, the court ruled that the district failed to offer FAPE to "a highly intelligent high schooler." Although evaluations showed that many of the skills of the student were at the elementary school level throughout high school, the school district asserted that it had provided FAPE because the student had passed all of his classes, many with good grades. The decision specifically pointed out that the fact that the student's "inability to write anywhere near grade level undermined the district's contention that it offered an appropriate program." In conclusion, the court ruled that because the school district failed to address the student's needs, the school district had to reimburse the student's parents for educational services they obtained privately. In doing so, the court invoked a key principal that school districts must provide "meaningful" educational benefit (see the Klein case for more information).

504 Plans vs. IEPs

Gifted students with disabilities may also be eligible for services under Section 504 of the Rehabilitation Act of 1973. Although IDEA is an education law, Section 504 is a civil rights law aimed at ensuring that all people with disabilities have access to any programs and services that receive federal funding. It applies not only to services during the school day, but also to services outside of the school day, such as a publicly funded homework club, sports activity, or drama club.

504 plans typically provide the accommodations that are needed by a student with a disability in order to have access to appropriate instruction. 504 plans do not typically include goals and objectives, do not typically involve any specialized instruction, and do not typically call for progress reports to be provided to parents on a regular basis. Although some parents may view 504 plans as being something "less" than an IEP, for many smart kids with learning difficulties, a 504 plan is all that is needed.

In order to qualify for or be eligible for a 504 plan under Section 504, a disabling condition must significantly impair one or more major life function. Specifically in Section 504, the law defines a person as disabled if the person has a physical or mental impairment such as blindness, deafness, or mental illness that substantially limits one or more major life activities. Under Section 504, a disabling condition does not need to be defined as one of the federally defined education disabilities. In qualifying for a 504 plan, the questions are whether the student has a disabling condition and whether it substantially limits the student. In contrast, the questions in an IEP determination are whether there is a disability, whether there is an educational impact to the disability, and whether the student requires special education services. All questions need to be answered affirmatively in each respective process (see Figure 2). IEPs deal with special education until the end of high school or the age of 22, whichever comes first. 504 plans can still be appropriate in postsecondary education and in the workplace.

Although the education of students with a 504 plan could consist of special education and related services, in practice it does not typically provide the direct special education that comes with an IEP. Although there is nothing in the law that prohibits a student with a 504 plan from participating in a special education class or receiving related services, 504 plans typically consist solely of accommodations. IEPs also contain accommodations, so there is typically no need for a student who has qualified for an IEP to also have a 504 plan.

The Office of Civil Rights (OCR) clarified the importance of 504 plans for gifted students with disabilities by saying,

> If the protections of 504 . . . are to have any meaning for a qualified handicapped person of superior intelligence, then the student must be entitled to implementation of a Section 504 Accommodation Plan which allows him to achieve educational success reasonably commensurate with his ability . . . (Durheim, 2012 p. 12)

In addition, some schools believe that gifted students, because they make higher grades in class, would not qualify for an IEP—an incorrect presumption. As the Education Center (n.d.) website pointed out, "Even a child with straight A's in a gifted program could qualify for an IEP" (Table 2, para. 4). This explanation is particularly helpful, as many gifted students

IEP Process Stage 4:
Eligibility Determination: ALL 3 MUST BE YES

Does the student meet criteria for one or more of the disability definitions?

Does the student's disability adversely affect his educational performance?

Does the student require special education and related services to address his educational needs?

Do not copy without permission from Special Needs Advocacy, LLC.

Figure 2. Eligibility determination questions for IEP process. Reprinted with permission of Special Needs Advocacy, LLC.

with disabilities may be bright enough to earn a high grade in a class even though their disability impacts their attention and/or behavior in that class. The deciding factor must be on how the disability affects the student's performance, not on the grades earned.

In 2009, Congress passed the Americans with Disabilities Amendments Act (ADAA). Several provisions in this act have helped gifted students with disabilities qualify for 504 plans. In the ADAA, Congress provided additional examples of major life activities that, if substantially limited, could be a reason for a student to qualify for a 504 plan. Examples of general activities that were spelled out by Congress include reading, concentration, thinking, communicating, learning, and working. Congress made it clear that this list is not exhaustive.

An important change in defining impairment in the ADAA is the stipulation that school districts not consider the ameliorating effects of any mitigating measures the student is using (e.g., medication, assistive technology, tutoring, learned behavioral modifications). This new stipulation now requires schools to consider what the student's performance would likely be without the mitigating factors.

In the ADAA, Congress made it clear that the determination of substantial limitation must be made on a case-by-case basis with respect to each individual student. Congress also spelled out that multidisciplinary committees must draw from a variety of sources. Although schools tend to rely on grades, Congress suggested in the ADAA that other sources and factors, including aptitude and achievement tests, teacher recommendations, and adaptive behavior, be considered.

All of these court cases, laws, and policies set the stage for providing smart kids with learning difficulties with access to appropriately challenging instruction. In December of 2007, Stephanie Monroe, Assistant Secretary for Civil Rights in the U. S. Department of Education, wrote her "Dear Colleague Letter: Access by Students with Disabilities." She discussed the fact that some schools and school districts had refused to allow qualified students to participate in challenging academic programs, such as Advanced Placement and International Baccalaureate programs. Monroe also discussed that some schools and school districts had required students to give up the IEP and 504 services that had been designed to meet their individual needs, as a condition of participation in challenging academic programs. She went on to make it clear that denying a student the opportunity to participate in an accelerated program based on his disability is a violation of federal law. In addition, she made it clear that students with disabilities must be able to receive appropriate accommodations and services while participating in these accelerated programs. We believe this letter removes any doubt that smart kids with a variety of disabilities must neither be excluded from accelerated instruction nor denied the opportunity to receive the accommodations and services that their 504 plan or IEP prescribes as necessary for their academic progress.

In conclusion, there are some important differences for the student in what may be available through a 504 plan versus an IEP. The IEP includes goals and objectives and provides a specific plan for direct instruction as needed. This direct special education is crucial for many twice-exceptional students. The IEP, like a 504 plan, includes classroom and testing accommodations. Unlike an IEP, 504 plans do not typically provide for special education instruction of any kind. They are administered and monitored by the general educators in the school, typically the guidance counselor. You should be aware that schools will sometimes be more willing to develop a 504 plan than an IEP, because the 504 plan will typically demand less resources from the school. For some students, the 504 plan, with its accommodations, will be enough to ensure access to appropriately rigorous instruction.

It is important to keep in mind that experts have estimated that as many as 2%–5% of all students are likely to fit the classification of GT/LD (Dix & Schafer, 1996; Whitmore, 1981). These figures have been substantiated in Montgomery County, MD, where 2% of all students have been identified as simultaneously gifted and disabled. As the National Association for Gifted Children (1998) says in its "Students with Concomitant Gifts and Learning Disabilities" position paper, "without appropriate identification and services, the gifts of these students may never be developed" (para. 6). We must continue to work to ensure that bright students with learning challenges have a fair opportunity to be identified as gifted. Secondly, as parents and advocates, you must continue to look at discrepancies between your child's gifts and his academic performance. Finally, you must insist that the difference between the potential evidenced by your child's gifts and the performance evidenced by her learning challenges be the first step that alerts others to the possibility of educational disabilities.

Response to Intervention

Response to Intervention (RtI) is designed to provide early identification and systematic assistance to students who are having difficulty learning in school. RtI is a collection of procedures used throughout the United States to determine how students respond to specific changes in general education instruction and to provide a process for data-based decision-making for creating, implementing, and evaluating appropriate interventions to improve student success. The core features of the RtI process are: (a) schoolwide screenings to identify students who may need additional assessment and/or interventions; (b) scientific, research-based, linguistically, and culturally responsive instructional practices and interventions matched to student needs; and (c) frequent monitoring of student progress. The delivery of services are divided into tiers:

- Tier 1 focuses on the instruction and interventions for all students in the general education setting;
- Tier 2 focuses on instruction and interventions for a small group within the regular education environment; and
- Tier 3 provides more intense intervention services within the regular classroom or outside of the regular classroom.

RtI plays a role in eligibility for special education. Before the use of RtI, some students were not being identified and, therefore, did not receive services in the early grades. RtI is designed to provide an earlier determination as to whether a student is in need of special services. Twice-exceptional students can be found in each tier, but their interventions need to reflect their high ability and individualized needs (Fuchs, 2009; Klotz & Canter, 2006; Logsdon, 2011; Reardon, 2009).

Response to Intervention (RtI) was introduced into the special education procedures as part of the reauthorization of IDEA in 2004. In the law, RtI was identified as a way to provide evidence-based instruction to students and frequent assessment of the effectiveness of that instruction. For the small number of students who would require Tier 2 or Tier 3 instruction, they could receive these interventions without necessarily being identified for special education. The identification of learning disabilities was changed in IDEA 2004 to encourage including the RtI process. The law stated that school districts would no longer be required to utilize the discrepancy model that had previously been the method of identification.

The move away from the discrepancy model caused great concern for many advocates of twice-exceptional students. With the discrepancy model, it was often very evident that a student had great aptitude as shown by his strong IQ scores, but might at the same time have educational achievement scores that were significantly weaker. The fear was that if school districts moved away from utilizing the discrepancy model, the disabilities of twice-exceptional students would more often be masked. Experience shows that this is especially the case in the early grades, as students may be able to perform close to or on grade level as they compensate for their disability. There was some relief among advocates, as the language of IDEA 2004 included a second alternative method of identification that gave school districts the option of looking at a pattern of strengths and weaknesses indicative of a student with a learning disability.

In practice, over the past years that IDEA 2004 has been in effect, there has been a national move to utilize RtI more and more, not only for the area of learning disabilities but for other disability areas as well. There have been several reasons for this trend. There are certainly many educators who believe that RtI is a superior way to identify students, as it provides evidence-based instruction for all students and does not require what has been labeled as a "wait to fail" model. Rather than waiting for a student to fail before beginning the special education process, RtI, when utilized correctly, can identify all students who are not responding to the general education interventions and provide them with more specialized interventions quickly. Colorado, under the leadership of Daphne Pereles, has established specific practices for utilizing RtI with twice-exceptional students (see http://www.cde.state.co.us/RtI). However, an article in *Education Week* (Samuels, 2008) highlighted the problems with utilizing RtI in areas other than in reading: "Although RTI has shown success with children just learning how to read, skeptics note that the research base is less solid for older students and students in other academic subjects" (p. 5).

Unfortunately, RtI has frequently been utilized as a way for school districts to delay the costly provision of special education services. There are many instances across the country where school districts have delayed or denied the evaluation process because the RtI process was still underway. Beverly Trail, author of *Twice-Exceptional Gifted Children: Understanding, Teaching, and Counseling Gifted Students*, writes that, "The intent of RtI could have positive implications, but the problem solving process has to involve experts who understand the needs of twice-exceptional students for the process to work" (personal communication, February 2012). Dr. Larry Silver, one of the pioneers of services for learning disabled students, wrote in the January/February 2012 edition of *LDA Newsletter* about the negative effects of RtI, including the closing of existing programs for students who might still need them and the expectation of general education teachers, who have not been adequately trained, to deliver services.

The delay and denial of the special education process has become such a problem that Melody Musgrove, director of the U.S. Department of Education Office of Special Education Programs, issued a memorandum on January 21, 2011, clearly stating that an RtI process cannot be used to delay or deny an evaluation for eligibility under IDEA. The memorandum spelled out that:

> It has come to the attention of the Office of Special Education Programs (OSEP) that, in some instances, local educational agencies (LEAs) may be using Response to Intervention (RTI) strategies to delay or deny a timely initial evaluation for children suspected of having a disability. States and LEAs have an obligation to ensure that evaluations of children suspected of having a disability are not delayed or denied because of implementation of an RTI strategy. (Musgrove, 2012, p. 1)

The memorandum goes on to specify that it is critical that the identification occur in a timely manner and that no procedures or practices result in delaying or denying this identification. The memorandum clarified that parents have a right to request an initial evaluation at any time and that the school district must meet to determine if there is reason to suspect a disability and proceed with the evaluation.

In a recent webinar from the National Association for Gifted Children (see http://nagc.sclivelearningcenter.com/index.aspx?PID=4241&SID=107836), Mike Postma, Dan Peters, Kathi Kearney, and Bobbie Gilman (2012) presented on the topic of "What Parents and Educators Should Know About RtI." The presenters, representing programs from across the country, presented advice and caution about the use of RtI in identifying twice-exceptional children. Some of the difficulties in using RtI for twice-exceptional students they noted were:

- RtI emphasizes identifying students that are performing below age/grade level expectations, which will miss many twice-exceptional students who perform at or close to the average range because of their ability to compensate or mask their difficulties.
- The complex profile of strengths and weakness of twice-exceptional children is typically only evident through comprehensive assessment.
- Even when twice-exceptional students are identified for RtI services, the services may be offered only until they reach the average range, when the expectation should be that achievement approaches ability.

As we consider whether or not twice-exceptional students qualify for services for their learning disability, we will need to use both the tools of RtI and an examination of patterns of strengths and weaknesses. RtI can be helpful in that Tier 2 and Tier 3 interventions can be implemented quickly without waiting for the special education process. It is up to parents and advocates to make sure that the RtI process truly involves the use of evidence-based interventions and that there is frequent assessment to see if the current intervention is working or if a new, more intensive intervention may be needed. Parents and advocates must be vigilant in calling for an evaluation if the RtI process is not meeting the child's needs. For many twice-exceptional students, it will be necessary to look carefully at their assessments for the patterns of strengths and weaknesses that are indicative of a student with a disability. This look at patterns requires an analysis of not just the full scale scores but also of the factor and subtest scores that often give us a clue of the isolated areas that cause smart kids with learning difficulties to struggle.

KEY POINTS

- Students who are bright and have learning challenges need to be carefully identified so that they can receive both the challenge and support they need and deserve.
- When we fail to identify smart kids with learning difficulties, there is a price for both our society and the individual.
- Behavior problems are sometimes the result of our not attending to the gift or the learning challenges.
- There are some important principles that, if in place, will ensure the procedures for identification are accurate and thorough:
  o schools should form a committee that represents classroom teachers, special educators, art or music teachers, and others including guidance counselors and media specialists;
  o effective screening and selection procedures should use multiple criteria including subjective and objective information, formal data, informal data, and nontraditional data;
  o children from different backgrounds and experiences and those with special needs should have a fair chance to be considered;
  o advocacy on the part of staff, parents, or students is a vital part of the process;
  o parents should contact their state department of education, as well as the local school district, for the current guidelines for gifted identification. The process for identifying disabilities is governed by federal law.

- Trust a high score. There are many reasons why a youngster does not perform well on an assessment, but there is only one reason why that student does perform well. He or she can do it!
- Use defensible screening practices that align with program goals.
- Observing and reflecting on a child's behaviors can alert adults to the presence of potential. Once the behaviors are recognized, appropriate responses may help that potential become performance.
- Children's behaviors are keys to our understanding.
- Our beliefs about students directly affect their achievement.
- Know the law. One promising part of IDEA 2004 is that gifted and talented students who are disabled were included in the groups of students whose needs have priority in the U.S. Department of Education grants to guide research, personnel preparation, and technical assistance. This is the first time that IDEA acknowledges the needs of twice-exceptional children. This opens the door for more attention and potentially more services to be provided for GT/LD students.
- Because FAPE includes requirement that IEPs should be aimed at the outcomes of independence and self-sufficiency, it may open the door to more targeted and comprehensive services for twice-exceptional students.
- When developing an IEP for twice-exceptional students, we must look beyond just the academic areas and consider the social-emotional and behavioral issues that may be impacting the student.
- When making determinations about whether a student qualifies for an IEP or 504 plan and when evaluating whether or not the student is making meaningful progress, schools must consider more than just the student's grades.

- Many new factors in the identification of students for 504 plans have made these plans more accessible for smart kids with learning difficulties.
- School districts may not exclude students with disabilities from challenging instruction and must ensure that the students with disabilities have the appropriate accommodations and services while in the challenging instruction.
- Students who have learning disabilities may qualify for an IEP. Another alternative for gifted students with disabilities is the development of a 504 plan.
- RtI may help students get the interventions that they need quickly and without necessarily being identified as a special education student.
- Looking at a pattern of strengths and weaknesses is included in the federal law as a way to identify learning disabled students and is often an important way to identify twice-exceptional students.
- RtI may not be used to delay or deny an evaluation for eligibility under IDEA. Parents may make a written request for an evaluation at any time, and when they do so, the school district must formally consider whether this evaluation is warranted.
- Advocates for twice-exceptional students should insist that, when RtI is being utilized, evidence-based measures are truly used, frequent assessments are being given, and that there is a timetable for evaluating data and adjusting interventions.

TIPS AND TOOLS

Supplementary materials included in this section:

> Identification Data Gathering Tools

> Recognizing and Freeing Potential Blank Template

> Report to Parents

> Response to Intervention

Identification Data Gathering Tools

It is critical that multiple measures are used to help us find our smart kids with learning differences. These measures tap into verbal and nonverbal strengths, reading and math abilities, and other strengths that kids share through their talents and interests. This information should be gathered from parents, kids, teachers, and community members who see kids from a variety of perspectives.

TIPS

Teacher

Find out the specific tools that are available to you when identifying students. Work with appropriate staff members to collect data about this student population. Learn how the data impacts instruction. Implement the appropriate strategies with students. Interpret the data to understand the instructional implications.

Parent

Find out the specific tools used by your school for identification purposes. When advocating for your child, ask questions regarding the tools that may be used for your child. Understand your rights within this process.

Student

Talk to your teachers and parents if you have questions about how the school learns what you know and how you learn best.

Identification Data Gathering Tools

Here are some examples of tools that can typically be used in identifying GT students:

_____ **Subjective and Objective Information**
- Verbal and nonverbal test data
- Teacher and parent checklists
- Nominations: parent, staff (school specialists), peer, student, community (coaches, music/dance teachers, religious teachers, etc.)
- Portfolios/work samples

_____ **Formal Data** (These tests are given by way of example rather than as definitive because individual instruments can change over time.)
- Achievement tests (California, Iowa)
- Aptitude/ability tests
- Nonverbal reasoning tests (Naglieri Test of Nonverbal Reasoning, Raven's Standard Progressive Matrices)
- Educational assessments (Woodcock-Johnson, Weschler Individual Achievement Test)
- Psychological assessments (Weschler Intelligence Scale for Children, Stanford Binet)
- Connor's Scales (Attention)
- Teacher checklists (Renzulli scales)
- Teacher and parent rating scales (SIGS)

_____ **Informal Data**
- Nominations from parents, staff
- Portfolios/work samples
- Teacher observations
- Preassessment data

_____ **Nontraditional Data**
- Community nomination
- Interview
- Peer nomination
- Student nomination

_____ **Potential Charts**
- ORR Charts

Recognizing and Freeing
Potential Blank Template

The everyday observations of behavior provide us with valuable information about our kids' potential. Parents and teachers can copy and fill in the following blank chart (or multiple charts, if needed) with specific examples under each of the six categories of the ORR process: thinking, responsibility, breaking work into parts, creative ability, appreciation of beauty, and interactions with others.

TIPS

Teacher

Learn and use the ORR process to gather additional information about students. Use the information to give students curricular opportunities to unleash their potential. Use the information as a hook for motivating students. Teach students to use the process in order to build self-efficacy and self-advocacy skills.

Parent

Learn and use the ORR process to gather additional information about your child. Use the information to give your child opportunities at home to unleash his potential. The information can act as a hook for motivating your child. Teach your child to use the process in order to build self-efficacy and self-advocacy skills. Gather information about your child and take it to a parent-teacher conference.

Student

Learn and use the ORR process to gather additional information about yourself. Use the information to give yourself opportunities at school and at home to unleash your potential. Practice an "I can!" attitude. Be a self-advocate and tell parents, teachers, coaches, and other adults who you are and what you can do.

Recognizing and Freeing
Potential Blank Template

ORR Category:_____

Observe	Reflect	Respond

Note. From "Potential: Winged possibilities to dreams realized!" by L. Barnes-Robinson, S. Jeweler, and M. C. Ricci, 2004, *Parenting for High Potential, June,* p. 20–25. Copyright 2004 by the National Association for Gifted Children. Adapted with permission.

Report to Parents

While gathering pieces of information during the identification process, use this form to summarize information in order to provide a clear understanding of an individual child's educational history, strengths, needs, and learning styles.

TIPS

Teacher

Work with parents to complete the form. Share with responsible staff.

Parent

Work with teachers to complete the form. Use as guidelines for next steps.

Student

Work with your parents and school staff to understand the information gathered about you.

Report to Parents

Student name:

Review of student records, including the following:

Recommendations for additional needed information:

Analysis of child's strengths and needs based on record review:

Information about specific educational programs:

Additional resources and related services:

Short-term action plan:

Long-term action plan:

Persons responsible for action plans and services:

Follow-up:

Response to Intervention

Response to Intervention (RtI) is designed to provide early identification, and systematic assistance to students who are having difficulty learning in school. RtI is a collection of procedures used throughout the United States to determine how students respond to specific changes in general education instruction and provide a process for data-based decision making for creating, implementing, and evaluating appropriate interventions to improve student success.

RtI was introduced into the special education procedures as part of the reauthorization of the federal special education law in 2004 (IDEA, 2004). In the law, RtI was identified as a way to provide evidence-based instruction to students and frequent assessment of the effectiveness of that instruction. The identification of learning disabilities was changed in IDEA 2004 to include the RtI process.

TIPS

Teacher

Use the graphics as tools for self-understanding of RtI and as tools to use with parents when conferencing about how you use and interpret their child's progress.

Parent

Use the graphics as tools for self-understanding of RtI and as tools to use with teachers when conferencing about how they are used with your child.

Response to Intervention

WHAT IS RTI?

Response to Intervention (RtI) is defined as "the practice of providing high-quality instruction and interventions matched to student need, monitoring progress frequently to make decisions about changes in instruction or goals, and applying child response data to important education decisions" (Batsche et al., 2005).

Batsche, G., Elliott, J., Graden, J. L. Grimes, J., Kovaleski, J. F., Prasse, D., et al. (2005). *Response to Intervention: Policy considerations and implementation.* Alexandria, VA: National Association of State Directors of Special Education. http://pbis.org/news/New/Newsletters/Newsletter4-2.aspx

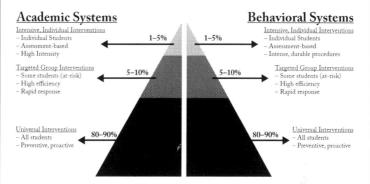

Academic Systems

Intensive, Individual Interventions
- Individual Students
- Assessment-based
- High Intensity

1–5%

Targeted Group Interventions
- Some students (at-risk)
- High efficiency
- Rapid response

5–10%

Universal Interventions
- All students
- Preventive, proactive

80–90%

Behavioral Systems

Intensive, Individual Interventions
- Individual Students
- Assessment-based
- Intense, durable procedures

1–5%

Targeted Group Interventions
- Some students (at-risk)
- High efficiency
- Rapid response

5–10%

Universal Interventions
- All students
- Preventive, proactive

80–90%

Integration of Academic and Social Behavior Three-Tiered Continuum of Behavior Support
SOURCE: Sugai, G. (June 23, 2001). *School climate and discipline: School-wide positive behavior support.* WATCH VIDEO at: http://www.youtube.com/watch?v=nkK1bT8ls0M

RTI: POSSIBLE PITFALLS

- "Tiered service delivery cannot be used to delay identification of students with disabilities; therefore, school personnel need to ensure that parents understand their right to request an **evaluation** as guaranteed under IDEA 2004
- The use of RTI methods upholds the parent's right to request an evaluation at any time to determine if a disability exists for their child"
  http://www.marylandpublicschools.org/NR/rdonlyres/FCB60C1D-6CC2-4270-BDAA-153D67247324/17125/Tiered_Instructional_ApproachRtI_June2009.pdf

Tool reprinted with permission of Special Needs Advocacy, LLC.

3

WHAT NEEDS TO BE DONE FOR SMART KIDS WITH LEARNING DIFFICULTIES, AND WHO IS RESPONSIBLE?

GUIDING PRINCIPLES THAT PROMOTE SUCCESS

What we do for bright students with learning difficulties is only part of the equation. *How* we do "the what" is just as important. In the right climate, where students know and feel they are respected and valued for their uniqueness, anything is possible. When students perceive they are devalued, the interventions, however appropriate, may fail. The goal of education is to provide opportunities for students to build knowledge, skills, and positive attitudes in order to become successful, contributing members of a global society. Successful, practical programming is based on solid research and theory.

 DOI:10.4324/9781003237983-4

These students must be guaranteed access to accelerated and enriched instruction that maintains the rigor and high standards expected of all gifted students. Bright students with learning challenges are therefore not to be excluded from this promise. Parents, keep this in mind when you review the information included in this chapter. Although much of this chapter is geared toward guiding teachers and the school system, you can use this information to your advantage—to advocate successfully for the school environment and experiences your child deserves and needs. You may also want to share the information and tools included in this chapter with your child's teacher.

Best Practices

The best practices for educating smart kids with learning problems can be summarized in four major components:

- instruction in the student's area of strength;
- opportunities for the instruction of skills and strategies in academic areas affected by the student's challenges;
- an appropriately differentiated program, including individualized instructional adaptations and accommodations systematically provided to students; and
- comprehensive case management to coordinate all aspects of the student's individual educational plan.

Research and a review of successful programs indicate that the most important component of these students' education is providing rigorous instruction in each student's area of strength. It is important that the instruction emphasizes problem solving, reasoning, and critical thinking, as well as includes extension and elaboration of the regular curriculum. Classroom organization must be flexible, yet structured with opportunities for collaborative goal setting, significant peer interactions, and cooperative learning. Students must receive this rigorous instruction in the least restrictive environment where they can receive educational benefit. In order to benefit from this instruction in a typical classroom setting, these students need educators to utilize appropriate strategies. Implementing these strategies involves close collaboration between special educators and general educators. By receiving appropriate instruction, these students can develop to their full potential (Baum, Emerick, Herman, & Dixon, 1989).

Smart kids with learning disabilities need instruction of skills and strategies in academic areas that are affected by the student's weakness or disability. Instruction is generally needed in one or more of the following areas: writing, reading, math calculations, organizational skills, test-taking skills, self-determination skills, and social skills. Research indicates that only a very small percentage of students are resistant to instruction that can greatly improve their performance in the academic areas affected by their disability. These improved skills allow GT/LD students even greater success in the development of their strengths. Skills and strategy instruction are accomplished through direct instruction and/or integrated into content instruction. Instruction in this area helps students to develop an awareness of their strengths and weaknesses and an ability to advocate for what they need in order to be successful.

Teachers need to adapt their program by utilizing a multisensory approach that emphasizes a student's strengths and interests. One successful example of this approach is the integration of art and drama into the curriculum within the middle school center program in Montgomery County, MD, that serves as a model for general education (see Chapter 4). An award-winning partnership with a local art college has integrated art and drama into all curricular areas, resulting in students demonstrating both a greater motivation and a greater mastery of the curricular objectives. An art specialist from the college works with teachers to identify key concepts in content areas and find ways that art can be used in both learning activities and assessment. In all of the Montgomery County Public Schools (MCPS) GT/LD Center programs, teachers use a similar process for integrating the arts.

Bright students who struggle in school need an appropriately differentiated program in order to be successful. Appropriate differentiation includes instructional adaptations and accommodations systematically provided to students (Maryland Task Force on Gifted and Talented Education, 1994; NAGC, 1998). Instruction and assignments should be structured in such a way that all students succeed to their fullest potential. Many resources for teachers detail appropriate adaptations and accommodations that obviate students' disabilities, allowing them to understand and present mastery of the material in a manner appropriate to their strengths. Utilizing appropriate assistive technology, which may include laptops, netbooks, tablets, portable keyboards, iPads, eReaders, audiobooks, Live Scribe pens, organizational software or apps such as Inspiration, word predictive software or apps such as Co-Writer or Word Q, calculators, speech-to-text software or apps such as Dragon Dictate, and text-to-speech software or apps such as Kurzweil 3000 helps GT/LD students to succeed. Methodologies such as team teaching allow students to participate in GT classes while receiving the supports necessary for them to be successful.

The final component, which is crucial for ensuring that all other components are in place for these students, is comprehensive case management. The case manager, most often the special education resource teacher, must utilize the skills of a wide variety of professionals to build a team that includes students and parents. The case manager must communicate with all involved staff regarding the student's strengths and needs, as well as the appropriate adaptations and accommodations. The case manager must coordinate all aspects of the student's individual educational plan, making sure the student is both challenged and supported.

Strength-Based Instruction

Regardless of the program model used, instruction must be geared to a student's strengths, rather than his weaknesses. The utilization of a variety of adaptations, strategies, and accommodations that allow GT/LD students to access gifted instruction is widely advocated (Baum, 2004; Baum, Owen, & Dixon, 1991; Silverman, 1989; VanTassel-Baska, 1991). When a student's gifts are identified and nurtured, there is an increased willingness on the part of the student to put forth greater effort to complete tasks (Baum et al., 1989). Our experience has been that this focus on strengths works equally well for students who are gifted and have ADHD or autism spectrum disorders.

Working through a child's strengths puts a positive spin on learning, especially for a student who has had continued difficulty in school. Instruction, when it is differentiated, better matches an individual's abilities, styles, and needs. Differentiation is a way of thinking and planning in order to meet the diverse needs of students based on their characteristics. Teachers differentiate content, process, and product according to students' readiness, interest, and learning profiles through a range of instructional and management strategies (Renzulli, 1977; Tomlinson, 1999).

Content is the subject matter prescribed by the state or district program of studies. For example, in social studies, students may be asked to write a research paper on the Civil War. *Process* is the internalization of information. Following the steps for the paper from notes, outline, and draft forms illustrates a process a student follows when dealing with the content material. *Product* is the outcome of the application of the processes to the content. The finished research paper is the product. Providing differentiation for these students, a variety of resources could be used to study the Civil War (content); organizational software and assisted note taking may aid in internalizing information (process); and the student may demonstrate her understanding through a model, dramatization, or Prezi presentation (product) instead of a research paper.

The following are examples of different ways to support strength-based instruction (Tomlinson, 2000):

- Study and practice models for gifted education (e.g., Creative Problem Solving, Bloom's taxonomy)
- Provide activities that focus on students' individual gifts and interests
- Provide open-ended outlets for the demonstration of knowledge
- Use differentiated instruction
- Provide tasks that fit students' learning style
- Provide multisensory instruction
- Provide guided discovery, especially when introducing new topics

- Give students choices
- Use collaboratively designed rubrics
- Provide hands-on experiences
- Provide real-life tasks
- Integrate visual and performing arts
- Vary content
  - Use multiple texts
  - Use varied resources
  - Compact curriculum
  - Provide learning contracts

- Vary process
  - Use interactive journals
  - Use tiered assignments
  - Create interest centers
  - Create learning centers

- Vary product
  - Provide varied modes of expression, materials, and technologies
  - Require advanced assignments that require higher order thinking skills
  - Provide authentic assessment
  - Use evaluations by selves and others

Simultaneously, in order for students to obtain the greatest benefit from rigorous instruction, programming strategies must exist that provide additional support in the areas of weakness. In order to help students succeed, teachers must provide organizational strategies and allow alternatives to writing as a means of communication. It is also crucial that the instruction emphasizes problem solving, reasoning, and critical thinking, as well as extending and elaborating the regular curriculum. Education of these children must focus on abstract ideas and generalizations (Baum et al., 1991). Differentiating rigorous instruction with appropriate individualized instructional adaptations and accommodations is necessary and requires close collaboration between special educators and general educators (Friend, 1996).

Understanding by Design

A template, Understanding by Design, was developed by Jay McTighe and Grant Wiggins (1999) for teachers to use in planning units and lessons (see p. 12 of http://www.grantwiggins.org/documents/UbDQuikvue1005.pdf for a copy of the template). We have found this to be a great tool for helping teachers to understand how to differentiate lessons for smart kids with learning difficulties. The plan for any lesson or unit requires that educators begin with the understandings, essential questions, knowledge, and skills that they expect students to know by the end of the lesson. Then the educator will plan how to assess students to see if they have, in fact, learned what the educator has set out to teach. Finally, the educator plans the learning activities that will allow each student to gain the understandings on which they will be assessed. What we emphasize is that none of the outcomes of instruction (the understanding, essential questions, knowledge, and skills) are different for smart kids with learning difficulties than they are for other smart kids. We do not "water down" or "dumb down" the curriculum. Instead, what we do is to differentiate is the way we will assess students and the learning activities we will provide.

To fully develop one example, the understanding that we have set for our smart students may be that they can demonstrate understanding of the causes of the Civil War. Rather than require that all students write an essay about this to demonstrate their understanding, we can instead offer alternatives such as developing an oral presentation, PowerPoint, or video. The expectations of the knowledge that would be demonstrated in these alternatives would be no different than what we would expect students to demonstrate through the essay. Similarly, when it comes to learning activities, we can provide alternative learning activities, such as viewing a video, listening to an expert, or reading a piece of text on an eReader. The richness and rigor of the information that would be presented in these alternative formats would be no less than what we would provide to students in their reading. When educators see that we are not suggesting that they lower their expectation of what is to be learned and demonstrated, and when we provide educators with alternatives of how students can learn and demonstrate information, they are typically more willing to provide what smart kids with learning difficulties need to access challenging instruction.

Adaptations and Accommodations

For twice-exceptional students who are gifted and have learning disabilities to effectively gain access to enriched and accelerated instruction, they often need to have appropriate adaptations and accommodations (Barton & Starnes, 1989; Baum, 1990; Cline & Schwartz, 1999; NAGC, 1998). Many accommodations allow bright students with learning challenges to demonstrate their knowledge without being hindered by the effects of their difficulties. In curricular planning, it is crucial that the teacher consider instructional methods and strategies that either circumvent the student's difficulties or build in the necessary scaffolding to empower him to be successful with the demands of the assignment. Again, this holds true not only for students with learning disabilities, but also for those with a wide range of learning difficulties, including autism spectrum disorders and ADHD.

Parents, when advocating for your child to receive adaptations and accommodations, it is essential to first understand the differences between an adaptation and an accommodation:

- An *adaptation* is a modification to the delivery of instruction or materials used, rather than a modification to the content being presented, as that can affect the fulfillment of curriculum goals (Lenz & Schumaker, 1999).
- An *accommodation* is a procedure or enhancement that empowers a person with a disability to complete a task that he or she would otherwise be unable to complete because of his or her disability (Maryland State Department of Education, 1999).

Students often receive inadequate or inappropriate adaptations and accommodations, making their access to gifted instruction problematic (Weinfeld, Barnes-Robinson, Jeweler

& Shevitz, 2002). It is natural for you, your child, and your child's teacher to have strong opinions and beliefs that influence which, if any, adaptations and accommodations you believe to be appropriate for your child. Some staff members will present you with a list of all possible accommodations to choose from as if it were a menu. Others may tell you which accommodations are appropriate based on their experiences with other students who may or may not be like your child. You may feel that your child is entitled to every accommodation available, and that no one at school is looking out for his best interests. Or you may believe that your child needs to be taught the basic skills just the way you were taught those skills years ago and that any accommodations are harmful.

In addition, some students believe that, because of their disability, they are entitled to have every accommodation possible, while other students reject the use of even the most reasonable accommodations because they think it might make them look different than their peers. Some staff members believe in providing any possible accommodation that will help a student do her best work, while other staff members think that many accommodations are unfair or harmful and are not preparing students for high-stakes exams, rigorous college courses, and the challenges of the real world. These differing beliefs and opinions often lead to either providing too few, too many, or the wrong accommodations.

Disagreement on the meaning and types of appropriate adaptations and accommodations for students is not only evident at the school level, but also at the state level. Although these policies relate to state regulations on formal assessments, they impact the accommodations that are allowed for classroom instruction and assessments. As teachers prepare their students for mandated state assessments, they often allow the same accommodations in their classroom instruction that will be allowed in the mandated assessments (Thurlow, House, Scott, & Ysseldyke, 2001).

Many accommodations allow students with disabilities to demonstrate their knowledge without being handicapped by the effects of their disabilities. Accommodations that are shown to be effective in research and practice are listed in this chapter's sections titled What Works and What Doesn't Work and Overcoming Obstacles.

A review of research literature (see citations after each principle) revealed the following principles as the best practices for providing appropriate adaptations and accommodations for these students in order to ensure that access. Following each principle is a discussion of what we have found to be the merits of each guideline.

- *Accommodations used in assessments should parallel accommodations that are integrated into classroom instruction* (Council for Exceptional Children [CEC], 2000; MSDE, 2000). During instruction and assessments, students should be allowed to access their strengths and truly demonstrate their knowledge. This is empowering, because the student is familiar with and comfortable with the use of the accommodation. In addition, introducing an accommodation for testing may only actually hinder a student who is unfamiliar with the accommodation (Tindal & Fuchs, 1999).

- *The adaptations and accommodations should be aligned with the educational impact of the individual student's disability and with the student's needs as described in his or her IEP or 504 plan* (CEC, 2000; MSDE, 2000). This principle relates to the idea of individualizing the accommodations for the specific student in question. Focusing on the individual student should answer the general educators' concern about whether the accommodation is needed by that student. The individual focus helps explain to the student what it is about her disability and needs that make it necessary for her to have the specific accommodations. Individualizing accommodations for the specific student in question is empowering because it is consistent with what the individual student needs at that time.

- *The adaptations and accommodations should be based upon the strengths of the student* (Baum, 1990; Gardner, 1983; NAGC, 1998). Consistent with the idea that working through each individual's gifts is the most important method to use with these students, an accommodation will only be useful if it capitalizes on a gift, allowing a student to circumvent his difficulty. This is empowering, because it capitalizes on the individual's strengths.

- *Accommodations are based on what students need in order to be provided with an equal opportunity to show what they know without impediment of their disability* (Thurlow et al., 2001). This is consistent with the idea of leveling the playing field that appears frequently in research on learning disabled students. Students should not be given an unfair advantage, but should be given an equal opportunity to succeed. Although individual potential varies from student to student, all students should be provided with the opportunity to reach their greatest potential. This should answer an educator's objection about students being given an unfair advantage and should also answer the student's perception of receiving an unfair advantage. This is empowering, because students have a fair chance to demonstrate their abilities, rather than giving them a crutch when none is needed.
- *Assessments allow students, while using appropriate accommodations, to demonstrate their skills without the interference of their disabilities* (CEC, 2000). Throughout the research literature concerning GT/LD students, it is noted how important it is for all students to be included in assessments in order to give an accurate picture of how all students are performing. Assessments that allow students to demonstrate their knowledge are empowering.
- *After selecting and providing appropriate adaptations and accommodations, their impact on the performance of the individual student is evaluated and only those that are effective are continued* (Fuchs, Fuchs, Eaton, Hamlett, & Karns, 2000). Evaluation provides data for deciding which accommodations are useful and should be continued. The evaluation answers an educator's concerns about having too many or unnecessary accommodations. It should also assure you, the parents, that selected accommodations are of value. It further demonstrates to students that only effective accommodations are part

89

of their individual plan. This is empowering because only useful accommodations are continued.

- *The adaptations and accommodations should be reviewed, revised, and when appropriate, faded out over time, allowing the student to move from dependence to independence* (MSDE, 2000). Accommodations that are no longer needed are removed over time. You, your child, and your child's teacher will see progress and growth, which is empowering.

- *A multidisciplinary team, which considers the input of you and your child, decides upon the adaptations and accommodations* (IDEA, 1990; Section 504, 1975). Your input, and that of your child, is considered, which is empowering. The professionals make the final determination and do not abdicate their responsibility.

- *The appropriate adaptations and accommodations and the rationale for each of them are shared with all staff members who work with the student* (IDEA, 1990). This guideline will mitigate objections from general educators when they see the rationale for each accommodation. Your child will be empowered if you are in agreement with her teacher as to what she needs and is capable of doing at that time.

In order to fully understand the strengths and weaknesses of a smart kid with learning difficulties, a comprehensive assessment is crucial. This is especially true for twice-exceptional students, because the gifts and challenges faced by these students often mask each other. Parents and teachers may doubt that the child is truly gifted because they don't often see evidence of the gift, especially when the child is asked to do things that are impacted by his disability. Conversely, the child may be doing well enough to get by, especially when the expectations are only that he get passing grades on grade-level material. It is often only when an evaluation is done by a skilled psychologist or neuropsychologist that we see the strengths and challenges that make up the profile of the gifted student with disabilities.

In a 2008 lecture, Dr. Julie Pace of Johns Hopkins University described the pieces that make up an effective evaluation. These pieces include:

- tests of overall ability such as IQ tests;
- tests of specific ability, such as achievement tests;
- cognitive processing tests, which reveal specific underlying areas of strengths and weaknesses;
- interviews with the child, the parents, and the teachers;
- a detailed history of the child's development and educational experiences; and
- observation of the child.

It requires a skilled evaluator who has experience with this population to understand the complexities of twice-exceptional children. Attention must be paid to scatter analysis, or the highs and lows that may make up the results of an individual test. When we look only at the full scale result, we may see an average score that hides both the giftedness and disability that are evident in the subtests. Parents have a right to an evaluation by the public school district when a disability is suspected. Parents need to make sure that the evaluator has expertise in testing twice-exceptional students, and parents may want to consider paying for an evaluation to be done privately. It is also important to note that parents have a right to an independent evaluation at public expense when they believe that the school evaluation was insufficient. Comprehensive evaluation is one of the first steps to identifying twice-exceptional students and determining what is needed in their educational program.

In summary, several key concepts emerge from these guidelines. The decisions regarding adaptations must be individualized for your child. The accommodations that are used in assessments must parallel those that are used in instruction and must be based on your student's strengths. The accommodations and assessments must provide an equal opportunity for your child to demonstrate her knowledge. And lastly, accommodations must be evaluated often and only those that are effective should be continued.

When considering adaptations and accommodations, the overarching principle is to move your child, over time, from dependence to independence. With that in mind, an accommodation that is appropriate at a given point in time may be replaced at a later time with another accommodation that helps him to be more independent. For example, an appropriate accommodation for a student who lacks keyboarding skills, but is gifted verbally, may be to dictate a composition. Later, when the same student has learned keyboarding skills, the use of a word processor may be more appropriate because it moves him toward greater independence.

Finally, these guidelines include principles of effective decision making and implementation. Although you and your child must have input into the process, the professionals must make the final decisions as to what is appropriate. There must be ongoing communication between the educators who are implementing these plans and yourself.

SOCIAL/EMOTIONAL PRINCIPLES

Mrs. Johnson received repeated calls from Charles' teachers during his fourth-grade year. They wanted to keep her informed about his unacceptable behavior. His behavior alternated between wandering around the room, often being loud and distracting, to sitting at his desk with his head down, refusing to follow the teacher's directions to "get to work." The teacher had tried many proven strategies—time outs, taking away recess, lunch detention, afterschool detention—but nothing seemed to work. Charles' mother wondered how it had gotten to this point. Charles had seemed like such a bright kindergartener and first grader, but over the last 2 years, his behavior had gotten steadily worse and he constantly told her that he hated school and felt dumb.

Mrs. Johnson was relieved when the school initiated the IEP process. She was encouraged when the psychoeducational assessment revealed that Charles had a verbal comprehension IQ score of 130, a very superior score. No one had ever considered Charles as gifted and learning how smart he was provided a great relief because the school now knew, too. But that relief quickly turned to apprehension when she learned that the school thought about placing Charles in a special program for students with emotional disabilities because of his behavior issues. Concerned, Mrs. Johnson shared the results with an educator friend who recommended that she involve someone who was an expert on twice-exceptional students.

At the next IEP meeting, the expert was able to help the team see that Charles was a gifted student who was avoiding reading and writing because of his learning disabilities in those areas. The expert pointed out that it was not unusual for gifted students with learning disabilities to develop emotional problems when their gifts and challenges were not adequately addressed. The meeting resulted in an IEP to target Charles's issues in reading and writing, while giving him the accommodations he needed to access gifted instruction.

In 2010, the National Association of Gifted Children (NAGC) created its Pre-K–Grade 12 Gifted Education Programming Standards. The standards indicate that teachers (and remember, parents are their child's first teacher) and other educators must understand the characteristics and needs of this population to be effective in working with and programming for their needs and services. These characteristics provide the rationale for appropriate interventions and services. They link the importance of affective development to cognitive growth, thus linking the characteristics of affective development to self-understanding and social awareness.

Let's look at two prevalent social/emotional characteristics in these students—perfectionism and emotional overexcitability—through the work of Annemarie Roeper, Kazimierz Dabrowski, and Michael Piechowski. At the heart of Roeper's work is the firm belief that emotional understanding is the key to the inner workings of the gifted child. To feel safe and to flourish, the whole child must be considered by fostering empathy, compassion, and appreciation for diversity (Roeper & Higgins, 2007). Dabrowski and Piechowski talked about the strong emotional reactions that are a critical part of the gifted personality. Dabrowski (1964) called these strong emotional reactions overexcitabilities, which he defined as above-average reactions to stimuli. Piechowski (1991) later found that parents were the first to notice these characteristics in their children.

One of the social-emotional needs of gifted children is to learn to deal with perfectionistic tendencies. Perfectionism is a characteristic that preoccupies the life of many a gifted child. There's the positive side that has kids wanting to do their best work, and then there's the other side that causes meltdowns from unrealistic expectations. A healthy dose of perfectionism can benefit twice-exceptional children by keeping them interested and on task to complete challenging assignments. Yet when things go awry, a youngster's disability may be getting in the way of performing up to high standards. If things get frustrating or too hard, kids may shut down by refusing to do the work or tearing up work that doesn't look good enough.

Parents and educators play an important role by helping kids set attainable and realistic goals while maintaining the challenge to meet high expectations. Helping students to understand how their learning differences can interfere so they can develop successful ways to accommodate or circumvent them will build self-confidence and self-worth while mediating the negative aspects of perfectionism.

In Figures 3 and 4, the ORR strategy provides parents and teachers with a way to understand the important characteristics of perfectionism and emotional overexcitability by discussing some of the behaviors that are observed, along with ideas for reflecting and responding to these behaviors.

Four other social/emotional characteristics to consider are self-knowledge, global awareness, moral courage, and empathy. In differing degrees, these characteristics are present in all children, but in twice-exceptional kids, their behaviors will manifest differently. In some cases these characteristics will not have emerged in our children and we will need to create opportunities for their development.

As we look to develop the twice-exceptional student's potential in the social/emotional realm, the ORR charts in Figures 5–8 (Barnes-Robinson, Jeweler, & Ricci, 2009) illustrate how parents and teachers can develop characteristics that will benefit their students by nurturing and supporting observed behaviors, along with ideas for reflecting and responding to these behaviors.

Perfectionism is a combination of thoughts and behaviors associated with high expectations for one's own performance.

Observe	Reflect	Respond
Sets goals appropriate to potential but other things, such as motor skills, may frustrate her if it gets in the way of her goal.	How can I help the student set goals that might be more attainable and not depend on skills that she may not have yet? Have I contributed to this frustration by setting unrealistic goals?	Together, set realistic goals. Explain that people cannot play basketball if they don't know how to dribble. If the student really wants to work toward a difficult goal, help her create a list of what needs to be accomplished first in order to get there.
Communicates that she "should" accomplish a specific task instead of "wanting" to do it.	Why does the student feel responsible for completing a specific task? How can I explore the "should" versus the "want" of doing things? Is the joy and passion for learning still there and does she differentiate between the two?	Have a discussion about things she likes to do. Together create a list of things that she likes to do and a list of things that she feels she should do. Talk about both lists. Explain that there are things that should be done in life but just as important is doing things of interest.
Is not always satisfied with her performance or herself.	Why is the student dissatisfied? What kinds of things cause the most difficulty? Are my expectations contributing to this issue?	Adjust my own behavior. With her, set more realistic expectations. Help her recognize and feel good about accomplishing her personal best. Help her realistically evaluate her tasks at school.

Figure 3. Perfectionism ORR chart.

Emotional overexcitability refers to an emotional richness in creatively and intellectually gifted children that is characterized by strong emotions and reactions to their inner conflict between the world as it is and the world as they perceive it should be.

Observe	Reflect	Respond
Experiences intense emotional reactions to people, ideas, and things	Under what circumstances does this behavior occur? Are there patterns that emerge? Are the reactions consistently the same or do they vary (e.g., temper tantrum versus isolation)?	Be accepting of intense feelings and help the student work through the problem. Help him recognize the triggers or warning signs when he becomes upset. Work with him to find coping mechanisms. Communicate with the parent to encourage consistent responses.
May appear overly sensitive in social situations.	In what situations does this occur most frequently? Are there specific things that trigger this behavior? Does it happen a lot? Does it manifest in the same way (e.g., cry, shut down, retreat, outburst)?	Brainstorm coping strategies with him when in these situations. Role-play some difficult situations and implement coping strategies at school after discussions with school counselor.
Blames others, objects, and events when things go wrong.	Why doesn't the student take some responsibility when things go wrong? Is there a pattern to this behavior? Are there some instances when he does take responsibility?	When a task is difficult, work with him to break it down into doable steps. Discuss what happens when things don't go according to plan. Reinforce that when things go wrong and mistakes are made, a caring person and support are there.
Is extremely active, energetic, and restless.	What is the student feeling at these times? What kinds of things cause the most activity? What are the situations where he copes well?	Identify times and places calm behavior is appropriate. Encourage and reinforce calming behaviors in difficult situations and help him apply and transfer the skills to less successful situations. Help him identify times/places when behavior is inappropriate by removing self from the setting (e.g., walk away, listen to music).
Asks probing questions; has a sharp sense of observation and searches for the truth.	Why does the student need to have answers? What are the issues he is adamant about?	Teach him ways to gather information. Teach him how to take different points of view. Model positive avenues of questioning within the classroom.
Has strong, emotional recall of past experiences.	Are the memories positive or negative? Were the emotions communicated at the time of the experience?	Monitor and be aware of strong emotional reactions to situations.

Figure 4. Emotional overexcitability ORR chart.

Self-knowledge is the information we have about ourselves that enables us to know and to work with our strengths and weaknesses.

Observe	Reflect	Respond
Enjoys being alone.	How does the student use "alone time"? What are her favorite activities? What are her strengths, interests, and needs?	Recognize her need for "alone time." Suggest to parents places in the community that foster her strengths and interests. Supply her with access to books and other resource materials to develop strengths and interests.
Tries new things alone before asking for help.	Is this because the student is confident? How do I help build confidence? Does she like to problem solve and take risks on her own? Why does she choose to try new things alone?	Encourage her independence. Talk with her about the qualities of motivation and initiative when they are demonstrated.
Has definite ideas about things; likes to share them.	When and where does this happen most often? What things matter the most to the child, and why? What influenced this idea?	Work with parents to access books and other resource materials to develop strengths and interests. Offer avenues for expressing ideas (e.g., write letters to editor, join a debate club).
Says, "I can do it!" Will take risks.	In what situations does this confidence surface? How do I reinforce the student's confidence?	Recognize her strengths and abilities by creating opportunities for her to demonstrate her competencies. Praise her for the "I can do it" attitude.
Advocates for self.	In what kinds of situations does this occur? How does the student self-advocate?	Talk about what being an advocate is all about. Explore where advocacy is part of some professions. Role-play situations that require self-advocacy.

Figure 5. Self-knowledge ORR chart. From "Pathways for Developing Potential in the Social-Emotional Realm," by L. Barnes-Robinson, M. C. Ricci, and S. Jeweler, 2009, *Parenting for High Potential*, p. 14. Copyright 2013 NAGC. Reprinted with permission of the National Association for Gifted Children. No further reprints are permitted without the consent of NAGC

Global awareness is the knowledge, interest in, and understanding of different peoples and cultures and the insight as to how we are connected.

Observe	Reflect	Respond
Shows interest in world events through reading, watching, and discussion.	What subjects are of most interest to the student? Does he feel some responsibility to get involved in some way?	Discuss the events with a goal to problem solving and understanding. Explore ways to make the global local.
Chooses to play with children from different backgrounds and cultures.	Is the student aware of any differences? What is it that attracts him to people of different cultures? What do I see him doing and hear him saying in these encounters? Does he like to learn from culturally different friends?	Talk about things we all have in common. Find school activities, international nights, and local organizations that are involved with different cultures. Help student identify resources that feature different cultures. Explore career opportunities that exist for people with these interests.
Is interested in the world around him.	What kinds of characters and parts of the world is the student interested in? Are there curriculum connections to be made? Do my students know their own family's history?	Give students an assignment that will help them to explore their family's history from geography to customs. Help them to create a sense of connectedness to other times and other people in other lands.

Figure 6. Global awareness ORR chart. From "Pathways for Developing Potential in the Social-Emotional Realm," by L. Barnes-Robinson, M. C. Ricci, and S. Jeweler, 2009, *Parenting for High Potential*, p. 15. Copyright 2013 NAGC. Reprinted with permission of the National Association for Gifted Children. No further reprints are permitted without the consent of NAGC

Moral courage is knowing and acting on what is right because of an inner conviction, belief, or principle.

Observe	Reflect	Respond
Objects when rules seem unfair.	In what settings do I notice this in the students? What specifically do I observe her doing and saying?	Talk with students about what criteria makes something fair. Make some house rules that meet our criteria. Analyze rules from local swim club, school, or other settings for fairness and equity.
Intervenes when children are being teased.	Why does the student get involved? What does she do? Does she stay safe? Has she assessed the situation accurately?	Talk with her about the feelings of those being teased and those doing the teasing. Brainstorm ways to intervene that keep people safe. Explore ways to eliminate teasing.
Argues for the "underdog" in a discussion. Shows empathy toward others.	How would the student describe an "underdog"? What issues is she most passionate about?	Ask her questions to help clarify and expand her thinking. Help her find ways to make a difference in the community.
Confronts peers when they are misbehaving.	When and where do I notice this? What approach does she take? What impact does this have on her peer relationships?	Talk with her about the means used and the goal of her interventions. Encourage her to think carefully and to take time to consider a response that will be positive.
Worries about the dangers in our world.	Where is the student getting information? At what level does she understand things? Are the fears realistic? Do I need to intervene and/or involve the parent?	Validate her concerns while helping to keep things in perspective. Make sure I know her sources of information, as well as the counter positions. Help her find local responses to global problems.

Figure 7. Moral courage ORR chart. From "Pathways for Developing Potential in the Social-Emotional Realm," by L. Barnes-Robinson, M. C. Ricci, and S. Jeweler, 2009, *Parenting for High Potential*, p. 15. Copyright 2013 NAGC. Reprinted with permission of the National Association for Gifted Children. No further reprints are permitted without the consent of NAGC

Empathy is the ability to understand and to feel what someone else is feeling and experiencing and to be able to convey it.

Observe	Reflect	Respond
Aware of how others are feeling.	In what settings do I see this most often? How does this awareness manifest itself in what the student says or does?	Talk about feelings and validate his sensitivities. Discuss the importance of thinking about our feelings and how hard it can be to talk about them. Discuss how this quality is manifested at school, and in the community. Together, analyze how this behavior is exemplified in literary characters, current events leaders, etc.
Quick to assess a social situation.	How does the student express this? Does he pick up on words and/or body language? Does he modify his behavior as a result of the situation?	Ask him to share the assessment of the situation, and how and why he reached certain conclusions.
Wants to help when someone is sad or crying.	How does the student help? Why does he feel a need to help?	Talk about different problem-solving strategies for helping others. Explore ways to give comfort, and how to react if the student does not want help. Explore volunteer possibilities.
Gives something to someone to cheer him up.	How does the student identify there is a need? What does he notice before responding?	Discuss with him the cues he is seeing in others. Talk about what can be communicated with words or gestures. Plant the seeds for a class project to help others.
Wants to give money or food to homeless people on the street.	What does the student know about the meaning of homelessness?	Talk about what it means to be homeless. Help create a class action plan to implement giving.
Wonders why a character in a story is sad or lonely or worried.	What does the student say and feel about the characters and is he aware of the relationship?	Discuss what event could happen in the story to change his feelings. Challenge him to write a story with a character who is sad, lonely, or worried.

Figure 8. Empathy ORR chart. From "Pathways for Developing Potential in the Social-Emotional Realm," by L. Barnes-Robinson, M. C. Ricci, and S. Jeweler, 2009, *Parenting for High Potential*, p. 16. Copyright 2013 NAGC. Reprinted with permission of the National Association for Gifted Children. No further reprints are permitted without the consent of NAGC

The social/emotional needs of smart kids with learning difficulties are as important as the educational ones. With few exceptions, social and emotional issues can contribute to a child's lack of achievement. It is important to see whether negative behaviors and attitudes are the result of an inadequate program or personal issues. For some students, placement in an appropriate program that attends to their gifts and offers support for their learning needs will result in a positive turnaround in behavior and attitude. The development of skills and competencies in the social/emotional realm contribute to and complement the other best practices that promote success. Social/emotional health matters inside the classroom and beyond. Students, your child included, need tools and practice to develop self-efficacy, or the ability to know and to believe in oneself. They need tools and practice for becoming self-advocates, or the ability to know oneself and represent oneself with others. For example, a GT/LD student needs to be able to approach a new teacher with necessary requests such as, "I can speak, but I have trouble writing. Can I give you this report as a recording?"

Students also need tools and practice to develop conflict resolution skills and communication skills. These are life skills that are essential for productive living. These are the skills that students need to help them make and keep friends, handle teasing, deal with anger and frustration, know when and how to ask for help, and get along with others at home and at school.

After students have had the opportunity to learn and practice using a conflict resolution tool as it is applied to a problem situation, they are ready for lessons that teach the curriculum using the tool. These curricular connections between the real world and the academic world reinforce and expand the application of what the students have learned. The goal is that students see themselves as successful learners by knowing who they are, what they need, which tools work for them, and how to get what they need to succeed.

INTERVENTIONS

Parents, when you or your child's teachers begin to suspect that she has learning difficulties, or even a specific learning disability such as dyslexia, the school should initiate a series of evaluation steps to determine if the learning problems exist and how best to accommodate for them. This section will discuss some of the evaluation steps schools should take to analyze and adapt for a student's learning problems.

When it is suspected that a bright or gifted student has learning challenges, it is crucial that the adults in his life meet with him to analyze his strengths and needs, and then together create an appropriate intervention plan. Creating this plan calls for analyzing a student's strengths, as well as his weaknesses. Next, the current program is evaluated to see how well it is nurturing and developing the student's strengths, while remediating, adapting, and accommodating for his weaknesses. Finally, recommendations are made for the program changes that will result in the appropriate level of challenge, and the instruction and support that will develop the student's gifts and strengthen his weaknesses.

Analyzing a student's strengths calls for a careful examination of both formal and informal data from both the school and the community. District and statewide assessments, as well as individual assessments, can reveal evidence of outstanding achievement. These assessments may include intelligence tests, achievement tests, and other screening devices that may be employed by the school for admission to specific programs or special schools. Again, it is crucial to look at subtest scores, not just at the broad overall scores, to see patterns of strengths and needs in order to view students in the best possible light. School classes and activities where students have shown exceptional interest, perseverance, self-regulation, or outstanding achievement must be looked at carefully. Finally, it is crucial to look at reports of the student's performance in community activities, including those from private instructors, coaches, peers, and the student himself.

An analysis of a student's learning challenges comes from a close look at test scores and how the student performs in different academic areas. Typical stumbling blocks that prevent students' access to rigorous instruction often are found in the areas of writing, organization, reading, and memory. Again, district and statewide assessments, as well as individual assessments and screening devices can yield important information about specific learning challenges that individual students may be facing. A look at the student's school history, as well as his current functioning across different subject areas will provide further evidence of the specific challenges that he may face. Some students meet the criteria to be identified with a specific disability, while others may not qualify for formal identification, but may still face significant challenges.

The final piece of analysis is to examine behavior and attention issues that may be preventing a student from succeeding in school. A thorough examination of these issues will look at performance across different subject areas at school, as well as performance at home and in the community. With this type of analysis, it will become evident which behaviors are a reaction to the current academic demands and which are more intrinsic to the student.

Once a student's strengths and challenges have been explored, schools should take a close look at the current program to see how well it is addressing both the identified strengths and challenges. Next, schools should explore the variety of supports, interventions, and instructional methods that are in place to both circumvent weaknesses and provide opportunities for strengthening them. In addition, schools must look at the special behavior management plans and counseling that are in place to meet the student's behavioral needs. Finally, the last step in the analysis is to look at the case management practices to ensure that all pieces are being addressed appropriately and that there is effective communication taking place between the school and a student's parents.

After completing a thorough analysis of the student's strengths and weaknesses and the current instruction and interventions that are in place, school personnel will make recommendations about adjustments in the student's program. These recommendations become the intervention plan that helps each student reach his or her potential. Most importantly, the intervention plan recommends increased opportunities for students to nurture and develop their strengths. These opportunities range from differentiated instruction in the classroom to participation in special projects and special classes or programs. As the obstacles are revealed in the analysis of student performance, adaptations and accommodations are built into the intervention plan that will allow the student to successfully access appropriate challenges. The intervention plan includes recommendations for the special instruction, behavioral/attention plans, and counseling support that the student needs to strengthen his weaker areas. The intervention plan specifies who is responsible for the case management and ensures that all staff and parents are functioning as a team to successfully implement the intervention plan. Finally, the intervention plan specifies how things will be implemented and who is responsible.

Bright students who have learning difficulties experience greater success when caring, involved adults and the student come together in a team approach to look at the student's strengths and needs. When his profile and his school's current program are carefully analyzed, interventions will be selected that will provide opportunities to develop the student's gifts, remove obstacles, and strengthen his areas of need.

OVERCOMING OBSTACLES

Smart kids with learning challenges often face stumbling blocks in the areas of writing, organization, reading, and memory. Specific challenges in each area include:

- writing:
  - o the physical act of putting words on paper
  - o handwriting
  - o generating topics
  - o combining words into meaningful sentence
  - o organizing sentences and incorporating adequate details and support statements into organized paragraphs
  - o revising and editing
  - o using language mechanics effectively (e.g., grammar, punctuation, spelling)
  - o spatial problems with organizing letters, words, or sentences on a page

- o remembering what should come next in writing in terms of accessing prior knowledge and organizing ideas
- o employing higher order cognitive skills as part of the writing process

- organization:
  - o following multistep directions
  - o planning the steps needed to complete a task
  - o organizing desk, locker, notebook, and other materials
  - o locating needed materials
  - o breaking long-range assignments into manageable steps
  - o prioritizing

- reading:
  - o decoding unfamiliar words
  - o inferring the meaning of new words
  - o summarizing
  - o reading fluently and quickly
  - o using textbooks

- memory:
  - o concentrating and keeping track of information
  - o quickly recalling details
  - o retrieving details after time has passed

Suggestions for appropriate adaptations and accommodations that work around student weaknesses related to these obstacles fall into four categories: assistive technology, instructional materials, teaching/assessment methods, and instruction. You may want to refer to the Bordering on Excellence tools on pp. 137–154 to efficiently and effectively differentiate content, process, and product in writing, organization, reading, and memory for these students. These materials provide specific suggestions for adaptations.

WHAT WORKS AND WHAT DOESN'T WORK

The following is a comprehensive description of what strategies and methods work and don't work for GT/LD students (Weinfeld et al., 2002). Although these strategies and methods were developed with GT/LD students in mind, they are appropriate for all smart kids with learning difficulties, including those with ADHD or autism spectrum disorders. This section encompasses social/emotional and academic recommendations, including specific strategies for each content area. Although the information is separated into different content areas, what works best for most of these students is an interdisciplinary approach. An interdisciplinary approach integrates thinking and learning skills and unifies content and process. This is important because students learn best when provided with information in a variety of ways. Parents, you will want to look for signs of these effective practices in your child's classroom and may want to share some of these practices with your child's teacher. Teachers of smart kids with learning difficulties can use these tips and suggestions to build a supportive environment for their students.

School Climate

Creating a comfortable, yet challenging classroom climate is essential. Addressing the social/emotional needs of smart kids with learning difficulties is critical to their achievement. The classroom climate should be designed to respect individuality, and accommodations should focus on strengths and potential for success, rather than remediation. A strong classroom climate promotes its students' development of an understanding of their unique strengths, empowering them to successfully advocate for themselves. Lowering standards, confrontational communication, and inflexible expectations that diminish student individuality is inappropriate in such a classroom. Instead, an ideal climate encourages interactive participation, flexibility, high standards, student participation in cooperative groups, individualized programming, active listening, and practice in conflict-resolution strategies.

The physical climate within the classroom should also be carefully orchestrated. A stimulating environment is ideal, with posters, collections, products, and highly visible student/teacher classroom standards and expectations for performance displayed throughout the room. Multimedia resources and technological tools, including computers, tablets, eReaders, tape recorders, calculators, and spell checkers should be available in a designated area in the classroom. In such an environment, students should have freedom of movement within the classroom. Careful attention must be given to both the physical and social climate in the classroom, creating an environment in which student needs are supported and abilities are recognized and nurtured.

Social/Emotional Skills and Strategies

At the beginning of the school year, teachers set the climate for collaboration, caring, respect, and negotiation for the year; good classrooms become a place where risk taking is encouraged and making mistakes is a way one grows and learns. The environment in such classrooms is not competitive, but rather a place where students measure their progress internally and receive a sense of worth and accomplishment from within.

Classroom rules should be established by the students in a spirit of fairness and an appreciation and valuation of individual differences. The rules should be posted in a prominent place and always referred to when problems arise. Problem-solving processes need to be formally taught and practiced throughout the year, and students are expected to apply them as needed. Students should use these skills in their relationships in school, as well as be able to recognize when these skills are used in literature, history, and social studies. These skills have real-world applications and consequences. The problem-solving processes should be posted in prominent places for easy reference. Many classrooms have a suggestion box where students are encouraged to share ideas to improve the sense of community in the classroom, including suggestions for classroom rules and processes.

In every classroom, conflict is natural, always present, and better approached with skill training to help students deepen their understanding of self and others (Jeweler & Barnes-Robinson, 1999). Suggested tools for handling conflicts include:

- *Active listening*: a process for hearing what is being said and understanding the message being sent. Students are able to paraphrase back to the speaker the content and feelings of the message.
- *Triggers*: understanding the verbal and nonverbal actions that can stimulate confrontation and anger. Students learn how to assess situations that cause conflict in their lives to better understand their relationship to the conflict (based on a strategy originated by Judith A. Zimmer of Street Law, Inc.).
- *Questioning*: a strategy to acquire, clarify, and synthesize information. Students' appropriate use of questioning strategies encourages higher level thinking and promotes good discussion (McAlpine, Weincek, Jeweler, & Finkbinder, 1982).
- *Brainstorming*: a technique to generate new ideas about a thought or problem about something or with someone. Students learn a process to accept and consider all ideas, before learning to evaluate and prioritize them.

Role-playing can become an everyday strategy to practice how to talk with teachers, peers, and others in order to build and sustain positive relationships. When a problem arises in the classroom, on the playground, at the bus stop, or in the lunchroom, all of the adults working with the students should take the time to process what has happened and utilize one of the problem-solving models that have been taught and practiced in the classroom. One example of a Creative Problem Solving model includes the following steps: recognize the problem, define the problem, gather ideas and data, rank ideas, test ideas, draw conclusions, and evaluate conclusions (McAlpine et al., 1982).

Another social/emotional strategy is the development of a growth mindset in your students. In Carol Dweck's (2010) research, she identified two belief systems that parents and educators hold that can have extraordinary impact on students' achievement. The first is a fixed mindset, which believes that intelligence is a fixed trait, and because we can't really change how smart we are, some students will always be smart, and some will not. The second belief system is a growth mindset, which believes that intelligence is a malleable quality, a potential that can be developed through effort and good instruction (Dweck, 2010).

In the last decade, brain research has expanded our knowledge and understanding of the brain's capacity to develop new ability. Learning about how the brain works is a first step for students in understanding how and why they learn and get smarter. The Brainology program at the Mindset Works site (http://www.mindsetworks.com) can help teachers with these lessons.

To get students thinking about how their brain works and how it can be changed, consider sharing information like the following:

> The vortex of the brain is comprised of billions of tiny nerve cells, and these nerve cells, or neurons, have branches connecting them to each other in a complicated network. What allows us to think and problem solve is the communication between these neurons. The more you learn, practice, and challenge yourself, the more your brain cells grow and the result is a stronger and smarter brain.

Here are some valuable things to say to help parents and educators send the right messages to children that will promote a growth mindset (Dweck, 2010):

- We believe in your potential and are committed to helping everyone get smarter.
- We value (and praise) taking on challenges, exerting effort, and surmounting obstacles more than we value (and praise) "natural" talent and easy success.
- Working hard to learn new things makes you smarter— it makes your brain grow new connections.

- School is not a place that judges you. It is a place where people help your brain grow new connections.

Instructional Skills and Strategies

Interdisciplinary approach. A successful curriculum method for twice-exceptional students will implement an interdisciplinary approach. In this approach, a variety of discipline fields including language arts, mathematics, science, social studies, and the arts are used for a student to examine a theme, issue, problem, topic, or experience. An interdisciplinary approach gives the student opportunities to integrate concepts, content, and process with learning and thinking skills. This approach is motivational and engaging for students as they deal with subject matter and abstract thinking. Differentiation is used effectively and efficiently using this approach. Students work in areas of strength and interests and the resources and materials chosen are at appropriate instructional levels that may range from abstract to concrete operations (McAlpine, Weincek, Jeweler, & Finkbinder, 2011).

Thematic units approach. Twice-exceptional students benefit when learning concepts and content through a thematic approach because a theme connects the objectives in each of the curriculum disciplines. For example, if students are studying Westward Expansion in a social studies class, they may be writing essays in English class, using graphs in math, and learning about butterflies in science. These students will enthusiastically gain an understanding of the topic through each of the disciplines (Shevitz, Stemple, Barnes-Robinson, & Jeweler, 2011).

Gifted instruction. Teachers, through training and self-study, can implement models for gifted education (e.g., Creative Problem Solving strategies and Bloom's taxonomy) in their classrooms. Teachers should use activities that focus on their students' strengths and interests, allowing for self-directed choices, and teachers should implement instruction that is multisensory with hands-on experiences. Guided discovery (such as KWL charts asking a student what he knows, wants to learn, and did learn in a lesson) is a powerful strategy used especially well when introducing new topics. Support and clarification for embedded directions, both oral and written, should be given to students.

Integrating the visual and performing arts into classrooms has been proven to be an effective tool for gifted education. Burton, Horowitz, and Abeles (1999) and Fisk (1999) found evidence that learning in the arts has significant effects on learning in other domains. Students are more motivated, and teachers report that students retain information more readily when the arts are integrated into the curriculum.

Gifted teachers should recognize that implementing remedial instruction and rigid task guidelines are not successful practices for GT/LD students. They should also never believe that learning-disabled students could organize their thinking without accommodations or instruction. Good teachers do not consider a lack of production a sign of motivational weakness or lower intelligence. Rote memorization, forced oral reading, text-based instruction, and the use of only teacher-directed activities are not used in successful gifted classrooms. Instead, effective teachers use instruction that works around weaknesses, provides for production of alternative products, provides real-life tasks, provides open-ended outlets for the demonstration of knowledge, presents tasks that fit the student's learning style, differentiates instruction, and uses collaboratively designed rubrics.

Thinking skills. Smart kids with learning difficulties are capable of exceptional thinking. Teachers should learn various thinking strategies, and teach, model, and practice these strategies in the classroom. Teachers should actively participate in the learning process using the Socratic method, a way of teaching using questions and answers that was practiced by the Greek philosopher, Socrates. This is a process that promotes discussion and responsibility. When this process is in place, students must come prepared for class, because they run the show. In turn, students learn to apply abstract concepts to everyday occurrences. Teachers can help students to transfer and apply the thinking strategies that work for them in their areas of strength to their areas of need. During the problem-solving process, teachers can use metacognitive skills and think aloud strategies to model the thinking process, or develop a thinking language to help students search for their own solutions. For example, a teacher may model a problem-solving process by posing an interesting problem and saying out loud what she is thinking as she solves the problem. Teachers should not assume that students already know thinking strategies and can apply them without ongoing practice.

Writing. The following was written by a twice-exceptional second-grade boy. Read it over to see if you can decipher what he is saying. What does this writing say about the challenges that this boy faces? More importantly, what does this writing say about his strengths?

> I wot to ocoplesh coleg an gat a doplom. To get ther worck herd an to get throw all finsh elomtre sclooh an mitol sclooh an hiy sclooh. Allworck hred an stote. Do me homewoark an sclooh work. I wel be abettor stodat To lor how to read tri hora book on tap. Todo my raed horak pratis. Read loto books beacu it in porto to read you wel ned to do it in ever job.

> Translation of the above: I want to accomplish college and get a diploma. To get there, I'll work hard and to get through, finishing elementary school and middle school and high school. I'll work hard and study. I'll do my homework and school work. I will be a better student. To learn how to read, I'll try hard and use books on tape. I will do my reading homework practice. I will read a lot of books because it is important to read. You will need to do it in every job.

Writing is often difficult for GT/LD students because many have trouble expressing themselves due to difficulty in organizing ideas, thoughts, and events, and giving attention to detail. Students also may have poor fine and gross motor skills. Teachers should focus on content more than handwriting skills and the quality of the ideas expressed rather than the quantity.

Establishing the writing process through discussion and practice is an ongoing activity in gifted classrooms. Using assistive technology—iPads, computers, electronic spellers, eReaders, apps, and organizational and word-predictive software—helps unlock a GT/LD student's ability to communicate what he knows and understands. Graphic organizers, mind-mapping strategies, extended time for completion of work, and clear written expectations for writing tasks help students create good writing products. And giving students prompts helps guide their purpose for writing. Rubrics, proofreading for one type of error at a time, and using a highlighter to indicate corrections aid in self-evaluation of written work. In addition, the publication of completed writing products for an audience serves as a great motivator during the writing process for smart kids with learning difficulties.

GT/LD students often have fine motor difficulties. Therefore, an occupational therapist should work with these students on handwriting instruction. The goal is legibility. Focusing on form, using mechanical pencils and grips, and using an appropriate handwriting program (e.g., Handwriting Without Tears) helps students who have difficulty writing by hand.

Lengthy handwriting tasks that result in fatigue and expectations that disregard a student's physical weakness or limitation are not effective methods for improving handwriting. Allowing students to use assistive technology, including an iPad, word processor, word-predictive software, or speech-to-text software, is often an appropriate alternative to handwritten assignments.

The administrators and staff of Bridges Academy (2011) in Studio City, CA, wrote an article focusing on dealing with anxiety as it relates to academics, particularly written expression (see http://www.2enewsletter.com/article_2011-09_writing1.html). Suggested strategies include:

- Establishing safe places through taking frequent breaks, verbalizing fears and frustrations, using noise-cancelling headphones, and engaging in role-playing, yoga, breathing exercises and stretching.
- Reframing wording by finding more student-friendly ways to describe writing, such as "authoring" or "producing."
- Developing trust between students and staff.

- Focusing on strengths and interests by integrating students' writing into a topic of interest and beginning by demonstrating understanding through their strengths.
- Puncture perfectionism by encouraging students to purposely do an example of their worst writing first before making a true effort on the writing task.
- Build confidence by providing one-on-one support, giving precise directions, breaking the task into manageable chunks, and providing specific times for task completion.
- Narrow the focus by not talking about the big picture, only the specific part of the task at hand.

Organization. Learning disabled students frequently have problems with the organizational demands of assignments. Teachers can help minimize the impact of this problem by structuring assignments with very clear directions and steps. Good organizational practices include establishing specific due dates and time frames for long-term assignments, providing checkpoints for monitoring progress, providing time for students to organize their materials and assignments, and providing a specific location for students to place completed work. Teaching students effective organizational strategies helps them to become more self-sufficient learners. The supervised use of assistive technology and visual organizers, as well as the use of the more traditional supports such as assignment books, study guides, homework hotlines, and calendars, all help students become more organized. Promising new practices for improving student organization skills include posting homework assignments on webpages, the use of hand-held organizers, and having students e-mail their own assignments to their home e-mail account.

Adults sometimes assume that students have the needed organizational skills, but are not using them because of laziness, lack of motivation, or poor attitudes. In the case of GT/LD students, this assumption is often not true, and such thinking can contribute to students' academic problems and low self-esteem.

Reading. Emphasis should be placed on comprehension of, listening for, and gaining pertinent information during reading instruction. Teachers must avoid focusing on word attack errors that do not affect comprehension. In addition, they should avoid using reading worksheets, round robin reading, and below-grade-level basal readers in their classrooms.

A successful reading program includes the use of literature for stimulating reading interest, oral discussion using supporting text, the development of expository reading, and the use of high-interest personal reading material that may be above grade level. Programs like the Jacob's Ladder Reading Comprehension Program, created by the Center for Gifted Education at The College of William and Mary, and the Junior Great Books program offer great opportunities for the development of reading and writing skills for students. These programs allow students to build on their abstract reasoning and comprehension skills. In addition to using these programs, students may also benefit from explicit instruction in phonological awareness, phonics, and decoding. The Wilson Reading System, the Orton-Gillingham approach, and Lindamood-Bell Learning Processes are excellent examples of programs and instructional approaches that have proven effective in teaching these reading skills. Accommodations such as digital books or text-to-speech software (which enables students to scan any print material and have the computer read the material aloud to them) are also appropriate supports to reading instruction. Many libraries have access to eReaders for their patrons and many tablet devices allow for eBooks as well. So many books of interest to children are available in eBook format, which should allow this accommodation to be easily made in the reading classroom.

Memory. Although students with learning difficulties often possess outstanding abstract reasoning abilities and are able to see the big picture readily, they often have difficulty remembering and sequencing details. When teachers motivate students through the use of a variety of modalities, they are much more likely to remember the details. GT/LD students are more successful when they can utilize assistive technology, as well as a variety of supports in the classroom environment. Students become more independent in this area as they learn techniques to enhance their own memory, such as mnemonics, visual imagery, outlining, note taking, and highlighting. Other successful strategies include having students sequence activities after a lesson or event, having them teach information to other students, providing environmental cues and prompts, relating information presented to the students' previous experiences, and telling them what to listen for when given directions or information.

Teaching in a way that requires students to recall details that are presented in a context that is not meaningful or does not incorporate a variety of modalities is not beneficial for these students. Once again, it is important not to assume that although these students have great ability in certain areas, they have learned the needed skills to circumvent their difficulties with memory of details.

Evaluation/Assessment. Students and teachers should collaborate on the type of evaluations and assessment methods and tools that will give an accurate picture of student understanding of both content and process material. Evaluations are based on instruction and reflect the attainment of the key concepts and basic understandings that are the focus of the curriculum.

Providing objectives, study guides, vocabulary, memory strategies, rubrics, and support and clarification for embedded questions aids students in accurately sharing what they know. Models of appropriate responses to prompts are helpful for students to use as a guide for creating their own responses. Differentiation in evaluations and assessments is important because evaluations must allow students to demonstrate their skills without the interference of their weaknesses. Accommodations to more traditional assessments include audiotaping responses, using a graphic organizer in lieu of paragraph responses, creating a model, or giving a speech.

Evaluations and assessments should be designed to maximize the student's demonstration of her knowledge of concepts and content. Lengthy essays, penalties for spelling in content areas, time limits, and matching tasks may not communicate a student's understanding of course material clearly. Attention should also be given to the formatting of evaluations in order to circumvent visual processing difficulties.

Mathematics. Preassessment of student mastery of mathematical categories (e.g., decimal fractions, whole numbers, statistics, probability) and objectives is an appropriate place to begin instruction. Focusing on developing conceptual skills and problem-solving strategies is essential, because these students are capable of higher order thinking (Bloom, 1956). Once they have learned a concept, they will be able to apply it to a novel problem or situation. Using interactive, hands-on programs (e.g., Hands-on Equations), manipulatives, and math tools help students grasp content and concepts. Students may need untimed tests, a reduction in the number of problems, and direct instruction in the use of calculators for accommodations to be successful.

Giving lengthy, repetitive assignments; having students copy from textbooks, overheads, or blackboards; or a focus on computation alone are not effective instructional strategies for smart kids with learning difficulties. Appropriate accommodations, such as a calculator, allow these students to utilize their often-superior math reasoning abilities while not being held back by their computation skills. For example, a student may be capable of mastering advanced math concepts, like algebraic equations, but can't remember how to do basic computations, like simple division. When given a calculator to use for the basic computations, the problem is eliminated.

Science. Science instruction that offers hands-on, interactive experiences is most successful because it involves students in the learning process, utilizing their strengths while working around their weaknesses in reading or writing. Activities that incorporate problem solving and real-life investigations with a purpose and an end product, along with a thematic approach that allows for students to direct their search for knowledge and answers, are meaningful to students because they are relevant and generated by the students themselves. Simulations and the integration of the visual and the performing arts are extremely successful when teaching science content and concepts.

Memorization of facts and emphasis on reading and writing are often counterproductive science activities for GT/LD students. The students may become experts in specific areas of interest when enough time is provided for them to do research projects. The acquisition of expertise through independent study enables these students to become valuable contributors to cooperative group projects. When researching a topic, the use of alternative strategies is crucial for these students.

Social studies. Social studies instruction is based on learning multiple facts and processing that content appropriately. Students should be responsible for learning the historical, economic, political, geographic, and cultural content standards. Students should be expected to construct understandings through systems of processing information, critical thinking, and problem solving. Thematic units, simulations, hands-on activities and projects, the use of various forms of media, integration of the visual and the performing arts, and extension or enrichment activities will help GT/LD students learn the necessary social studies concepts. Instruction led by textbook reading and focusing on memorization of facts, rather than understanding the concepts, is not an effective learning strategy for these students. For example, a student may not be able to write about ancient Greece, but can participate in a simulation of the political processes of ancient Greece to demonstrate his understanding.

ROLES AND RESPONSIBILITIES

The following is an analysis of the roles and responsibilities of those involved in the education of smart kids with learning difficulties.

Administrator/Principal

The school administrator must create a school climate that fosters respect for individuals and ideas, innovation, and openness to different learning styles and teaching methodologies required to reach these students. The administrator should provide ongoing explanations to school staff, parents, and community members about programs and services for gifted/learning disabled students. The administrator should model a collaborative approach for discipline that empowers students and teaches them to use conflict resolution and Creative Problem Solving strategies. By using a conflict resolution model, students have the opportunity to employ their excellent cognitive skills while simultaneously developing their intrapersonal and interpersonal skills.

The principal, as the instructional leader, should know every student in the building and offer support to the teachers in meeting the needs of each student. Interventions include allocating appropriate support staff; creating scheduling options; ordering appropriate materials and resources, including technology; and providing guidance for the creation and utilization of appropriate adaptations and accommodations for students. The administrator is also responsible for coordinating meetings to plan for implementing both gifted instruction and special education instruction that will enable each student to succeed to his or her fullest potential. The administrator also coordinates the required IEP or 504 team process for identified gifted students with disabilities and ensures the implementation of their plans. The principal must make sure that the best practices for educating all bright kids with learning challenges occurs. He or she also monitors the inclusion of learning disabled students in all school events so that they are an integral part of the school community.

General Educator

The general education classroom teacher needs to recognize and accept that these students are gifted first and disabled second and to understand that they need to be viewed primarily in terms of their giftedness. Therefore, the program in general education classrooms should focus on developing and utilizing the strengths of the student—not only on remediating weaknesses. Teachers should provide strategies that circumvent students' deficits, empowering these students to participate in the same rigorous curriculum as other gifted children. As a result, students are immersed in a climate that promotes self-efficacy and a solid sense of self-sufficiency, while being provided with instruction that demands the use of their gifted abilities.

More and more classrooms, schools, and school districts are embracing the concept of universal design. The Universal Design for Learning (UDL) educational framework relies on three principles to guide teachers as they use technology and other means to reach students with different learning styles, such as twice-exceptional students. The principles of UDL include (Rose & Gravel, 2010):

- Provide multiple, flexible methods of **presentation** that give students various ways to acquire information.
- Provide multiple, flexible methods of **expression** that offer students alternatives for demonstrating what they know.
- Provide multiple, flexible options for **engagement** to help students get interested, be challenged, and stay motivated.

What makes universal design very special is that it is in place in the classroom for all students, so no one feels singled out or embarrassed about their differences. It has been compared with making a building accessible to those with physical disabilities when it is built rather than trying to deal with an inaccessible building after the fact.

The general educator can nurture giftedness in numerous ways. He or she can provide necessary accommodations for these students while ensuring the appropriate level of acceleration and enrichment by differentiating instruction throughout its content, process, and product expectations. Teachers must allow students to see the big picture and state objectives clearly so that students know what is expected. Students should be exposed to advanced materials and concepts that require them to make connections and extensions to knowledge previously obtained. Within the advanced content, teachers should have students go beyond the factual information to analyze, interpret, evaluate, create, and make connections. Teachers should compact the curriculum to free up time for advanced levels of instruction. The use of simulations and open-ended questions also provides students with opportunities to engage in higher level thinking skills. Students are taught strategies to circumvent deficits. One example is using a mnemonic device (such as HOMES for the Great Lakes: Huron, Ontario, Michigan, Erie, Superior) to help with memory issues. In addition, technology tools should be made available in general education classes to accommodate a student's needs.

Teachers should encourage students to take responsibility and ownership for the decisions made about their education. In completing tasks and assignments, students are provided with choices to demonstrate their knowledge and understanding of concepts and content. By maintaining high expectations and standards in an atmosphere of support, humor, and comfort, teachers help students grow academically and love learning.

The general educator also keeps the lines of communication open between students, staff, and parents and guardians. When all parties work respectfully to establish open and direct communication, a lasting partnership is possible.

Special Educators

Special education resource teachers, speech and language therapists, occupational therapists, paraeducators, and all staff working with the student with disabilities are part of the team of school professionals responsible for learning disabled students receiving needed services.

The resource teacher acts as a case manager, monitoring the program, accommodations, and progress of the student. He or she also teaches the student strategies and skills he needs to access gifted instruction. These may include using reading, writing, organization, and memory aids, as well as self-advocacy skills and other social skills. Through direct instruction, the resource teacher teaches the strategies to develop skills that remedy the academic problems affected by the student's disability. For many students with disabilities, their only special education intervention consists of one class period each day with the resource teacher. The special education resource teacher not only works with students with disabilities, but also works with the school's staff to help them develop an understanding of how to meet the instructional needs of learning disabled children while not reducing intellectual expectations. The special education resource teacher also maintains ongoing communication with parents.

School Counselor

The school counselor plays a vital, multifaceted role in helping to provide an enriching, nurturing, and supportive school climate for these students. By the time these children are correctly identified and an appropriate learning environment is provided, they have often experienced failure, both academically and socially. The counselor helps students develop an accurate understanding of their strengths and needs. These students are bright and perceptive and can see through interventions that are not genuine and respectful. An environment where they experience success and are surrounded by people who value them for who they are is essential for their continued success.

The counselor supports the program by coordinating and sharing information with the school team to help them understand the unique characteristics of the students. Information is shared through in-service sessions, team meetings, individual meetings, and meetings with the principal. The counselor works with staff to ensure that appropriate adaptations and accommodations are made for students and that the child's individual program is well-coordinated. There is a danger that smart kids with learning difficulties will have either their giftedness or their areas of need addressed in isolation. The challenge is to simultaneously serve these kids in both dimensions. In addition, the counselor helps the staff clarify the rules and expectations for each setting the student will likely encounter.

The counselor meets with students with disabilities individually, in small groups, in the whole class, and in informal settings regarding issues and concerns. The counselor meets with students who come to see her on their own accord, as well as those who come at the suggestion of a parent or teacher. Sometimes, counselors conduct class meetings and give social skills training to students that includes topics like dealing with disappointments, coping strategies, making and keeping friends, clarifying rules and expectations, risk taking in social settings, and asking for help. The counselor helps students to develop a full understanding of their unique strengths and needs. This sets the stage for students to learn which adaptations and accommodations are effective for them, allowing them to become self-advocates. The counselor becomes an advocate for students when they feel they cannot fend for themselves. The counselor should also encourage students to participate in school clubs, activities, teams, and organizations. Counseling interventions often set the tone for the school's positive acceptance of bright underachieving kids, including gifted students with disabilities.

The counselor's role also includes communicating with you, the parents of these students, individually and within parenting groups. Through participation in a partnership, counselors can help you learn to accept and value your children for who they are and will more than likely encourage you to become involved with organizations that serve and represent your learning disabled child.

Mentors

Mentors inspire! This was the definition that was offered by a fourth-grade student participating in a local mentor program. Mentoring, either through a formal mentor program or informally by a single staff member or parent volunteer matched to a student, may be one of the most powerful tools you can provide for GT/LD students and one of the easiest to implement. Giving students the opportunity to work one-on-one with a mentor offers an optimum match and an ideal climate for bright students with learning challenges by providing an opportunity to focus on their strengths and potential for success, rather than their lack of achievement in specific areas. Mentors who are sensitive to students' needs and who offer positive reinforcement of students' efforts and accomplishments are able to help them realize their creative and intellectual potential.

Two of the most important components of a successful mentor program are the one-on-one mentor-to-student relationship and the opportunity to pursue an area of interest to the student. The mentor serves to validate the student as a successful learner, increasing her self-concept.

Many of the learning problems that manifest themselves in the regular classroom are not apparent when working with a mentor. Poor organizational skills and lack of follow-though are also minimized when the student is working with a mentor who is able to provide the individual attention and needed guidance and support to be successful. It has been shown that students show strong task commitment and motivation when the topic is personally meaningful (Baum, 1984; Baum et al., 1991; Shevitz, Weinfeld, Jeweler, & Barnes-Robinson, 2003). Therefore, motivation is increased when a mentor provides the student with the opportunity to select a topic of interest. In addition, in the regular classroom, many assignments require large amounts of reading and writing, areas that often cause difficulty for these students. A mentor program that is designed to allow for alternative products enables students to gain awareness of their capabilities and learning styles. Although having a final product at the end of the program is an accomplishment for which they are proud, it is the relationship that develops with the mentor that students repeatedly claim is the best part of the mentor program.

Mentors must be carefully screened and selected based on their knowledge in a specific field and their eagerness to share their skills with young people. Through the unique one-to-one relationship, the mentors are able to help the students pursue a passion, while guiding them in developing skills necessary to succeed in school. For some students, the mentor program is the only programming necessary in order for the student to be provided the boost that he or she needs to gain confidence and be successful. (For a description of a successful mentor program, see Chapter 4.)

MENTOR is a national organization dedicated to supporting and providing resources for mentor programs across the country. Its website, http://www.Mentor.org, offers a wealth of resources for anyone wanting to create a mentor program as well as training and support for a program already established. In addition, it maintains an online service that provides an avenue to connect individuals interested in mentoring to mentor programs/opportunities in their area.

Students

Your child needs to be empowered as he becomes involved in his learning. Once provided with tools, strategies, and skills for learning, your child can successfully develop and use his intellect. Students have responsibilities as learners. In order to be successful, your child must recognize and accept both his strengths and needs and gain an understanding of how he learns best (metacognition). Once aware of his specific issues, he can become active in learning and practicing strategies for thinking, organization, communication, problem solving, and the use of technology. Students are expected to eventually complete assignments independently, become self-directed, and seek help and support as needed. Learning and practicing strategies for developing self-efficacy (the belief in self) and self-advocacy (the ability to tell others what is needed) make it possible for these students to become risk takers and lifelong learners. Over time, students develop the skills and maturity that allow them to become partners in making decisions regarding their IEPs.

Parents/Guardian

Parents are usually the most active advocates for smart kids with learning difficulties. Children are often identified as gifted or as gifted/learning disabled because their parents or guardians have noticed the strengths of their children in their home environment. Parents, you should become teammates along with your child and the education professionals at her school in creating a successful learning experience for her.

You can support your child's success in school in a number of ways. You should maintain an open attitude toward instruction and school and help your child realize that school is her job and a gateway to life achievement. You know your child's strengths and needs and should help your child to understand them. You must also help your child understand and actively attempt to meet her goals, including those in the IEP, 504 plan, and less formal plans.

You should communicate with your student and the school staff on a variety of issues, including progress and planning. You can help your child focus on school assignments and, at the same time, empower your student to accept responsibility for his own learning. You can transfer strong advocacy skills to your child and reinforce thinking and leadership skills learned at school. You may be able to facilitate communication between school staff and other personnel in the community, such as doctors, therapists, and tutors who may be working with your child. You should also implement suggestions for parenting techniques that foster the development of self-esteem and self-efficacy to provide consistency and continuity between a child's home and school experiences.

KEY POINTS

- The best practices for educating these students can be summarized in four major components:
  o instruction in the student's area of strength;
  o opportunities for the instruction of skills and strategies in academic areas that are affected by the student's challenges;
  o an appropriately differentiated program, including individualized instructional adaptations and accommodations systematically provided to students; and
  o comprehensive case management to coordinate all aspects of the student's individual educational plan.

- Regardless of the program model used, the instruction must be geared to a student's strengths, rather than her weaknesses.
- Simultaneously, in order for students to obtain the greatest benefit from rigorous instruction, programming strategies must exist that provide additional support in their areas of weakness.
- An interdisciplinary approach integrates thinking and learning skills and unifies content and process.
- Twice-exceptional students learn best when there is an overarching theme or concept that connects the learning objectives among the disciplines.
- For twice-exceptional students to effectively gain access to enriched and accelerated instruction, they often need to have appropriate adaptations and accommodations.

- o The decisions regarding adaptations must be individualized for each student.
- o The accommodations that are used in assessments must parallel those that are used in instruction and must be based on student strengths.
- o The accommodations and assessments must provide an equal opportunity for students to demonstrate their knowledge.
- o The accommodations must be evaluated often and only those that are effective should be continued.

- The social/emotional needs of these students are as important as the educational ones.
- Understand perfectionism and emotional overexcitability.
- Understand fixed and growth mindsets:
  - o Intelligence is not fixed and we can change how smart we are.
  - o Practice and challenge grow a smarter brain.
  - o Praise for effort not intelligence.

- Students also need tools and practice to develop conflict resolution skills and communication skills.
- When it is suspected that a student is a bright or gifted student who has learning challenges, it is crucial that the adults who are involved come together with the student to analyze the student's strengths and needs and then together create an appropriate intervention plan.
- These students often face stumbling blocks in the areas of writing, organization, reading, and memory.
- Teachers, students, and parents must be aware of the specific strategies and methods that work and don't work for GT/LD students.

- Teachers need training to understand that there are many alternative ways for students to learn information and to demonstrate their understanding and that using these alternatives does not "water down" or "dumb down" the curriculum.
- Use updated technology in the classroom for instruction and teach students how to use assistive technology.
- Universal Design for Learning is a promising practice that removes the obstacles to accessing instruction for all students as an instructional practice that is built into all curriculum planning.
- Roles and responsibilities must be clearly defined.
- The mentor/student relationship can serve as a catalyst for improving the student's view of himself and empower him to be successful in the classroom.

TIPS AND TOOLS

Supplementary materials included in this section:

- ➤ What Works/What Doesn't Work Charts
- ➤ Bordering on Excellence Tools
- ➤ Differentiation Checklist
- ➤ Differentiation Pyramid
- ➤ Assistive Technology Options
- ➤ Academic ORR
- ➤ Who's Who: Roles and Responsibilities

What Works/What Doesn't Work Charts

The following are charts of what works and what doesn't work for bright kids with learning difficulties.

TIPS

Teacher

Use as a self-evaluation checklist. Use charts when planning for instruction. Use as a communication tool with parents, other staff members, and students.

Parent

Use as an evaluation tool of your child's school experience. Use it for creating questions to ask at conferences. Work with your child to implement what works and what doesn't work regarding homework.

Student

Ask your teacher and parent about what works and what doesn't work for you. Use the chart information when practicing self-advocacy skills.

What Works/What Doesn't Work Charts

Area of Concern	What Works	What Doesn't Work
Climate	• Understanding of student's unique strengths and needs • Promoting self-advocacy skills • Comfortable, yet challenging classroom with a stimulating environment—posters, collections, and products displayed • Highly visible class standards and expectations • Student freedom of movement within classroom • Interactive participation • Flexibility • High classroom standards • Cooperative groups • Individualized programming • Conflict resolution instruction • Multimedia resources available • Technological tools available—word processors, calculators, spell checkers	• Routine and remedial drill and practice with focus on students' disabilities • Lowering standards • Confrontational communication • Inflexible expectations that diminish student individuality
Social/Emotional	• Offering alternative ideas and options • Extracurricular enrichment activities • Teaching students to channel frustrations • Easing and removing barriers and planning for the future • Using nonverbal strategies to support students • Discipline as a teachable moment • Encouraging risk taking	• Disrespect • Sarcasm • Limiting options and choices • Stressing the importance of the weaknesses • Using negative consequences only • Using one instructional method • Denying access to positive learning experiences

What Works/What Doesn't Work Charts, continued

Area of Concern	What Works	What Doesn't Work
Social/Emotional, continued	• Opportunities to practice skills to build confidence • Respecting students • Encouragement • Connecting to students through their strengths and interests • Focusing on strengths, analyzing successes, and applying strengths to weaknesses • Teaching conflict resolution skills • Teaching self-advocacy and self-efficacy • Offering choices	• Discipline as punishment only • Lack of communication • Fear of being wrong or making mistakes
Gifted Instruction	• Studying, knowing, and practicing models for gifted education • Activities that focus on students' gifts and interests • Open-ended outlets for the demonstration of knowledge • Differentiated instruction • Tasks that fit student's learning styles • Multisensory instruction • Support and clarification for directions • Offering students choices • Alternative product options • Collaboratively designed rubrics • Hands-on experiences • Real-life tasks • Integration of visual and performing arts	• Remedial instruction • Rigid task guidelines • Belief that GT/LD students can organize their thinking without accommodations or instruction • Perceiving lack of production as a sign of motivational weakness or lower intelligence • Rote memorization • Forced oral reading • Text-based instruction • Only teacher-directed activities (lecture only; activities that do not encourage student decision making or participation)

What Works/What Doesn't Work Charts, continued

Area of Concern	What Works	What Doesn't Work
Thinking	• Teachers learning thinking strategies • Teaching and modeling thinking strategies • Practicing thinking strategies in the classroom • Applying thinking strategies • Working with GT/LD students to formulate questions, think through problems, use the Socratic method, actively participate in the learning process, apply abstract concepts to everyday occurrences, develop a thinking process, develop a thinking language, or search for their own solutions • Utilizing metacognitive skills • Transferring/applying thinking strategies that work in areas of strengths to areas of need	• Assuming students know thinking strategies • Assuming students can apply thinking strategies without ongoing practice
Reading	• Emphasis on comprehension, and gaining information • Using literature for stimulating reading interests • High-interest personal reading material • Programs like the William and Mary Reading Program that build abstract reasoning and comprehension skills • Development of expository reading • Oral discussion using supporting text • Explicit instruction in phonological awareness, phonics, and decoding (such as that used in Wilson Reading Program) • Using books on tape and speech-to-text software	• Focusing on errors that do not affect comprehension • Reading worksheets • Round-robin reading • Categorizing below–grade-level basal readers

What Works/What Doesn't Work Charts, continued

Area of Concern	What Works	What Doesn't Work
Writing	• Establishing writing process through ongoing discussion and practice • Assistive technology—portable word processors, computers, electronic spellers, word-predictive software • Graphic organizers • Mind mapping strategies • Extended time for completion of work • Clearly written expectations for writing tasks • Writing prompts • Proofreading for one type of error at a time • Highlighters to indicate corrections • Publication of writing for an audience	• Focusing on handwriting instead of content • Quantity versus quality • Using red pens to denote errors
Organization	• Electronic organizers • Software organization programs • Study guides that help locate information and answers • Assignment books and calendars for recording assignments • Graphic organizers—outlines, webs, diagrams, storyboards • Establishing specific due dates for short assignments and time frames for long-term assignments • Breaking up tasks into workable and obtainable steps • Providing checkpoints for long-term assignments and monitoring progress frequently • Providing time to organize materials and assignments • Providing a homework hotline or Web page • A specific location for students to place completed work	• Assuming students have the needed organizational skills • Attributing poor organizational skills to lack of motivation, bad attitude, or laziness • Assigning long-term or complicated assignments without supports for organization • Expecting students to utilize organizational supports without providing instruction in the use of those supports

What Works/What Doesn't Work Charts, continued

Area of Concern	What Works	What Doesn't Work
Organization, continued	• Monitoring students' accuracy in recording assignments and/or providing printed copy. • Multiple modalities when presenting directions, explanations, and instructional content • Having students sequence activities after a lesson or event	
Memory	• Providing students with a copy of the information that highlights key facts • Having students tape record directions or information • Providing students with environmental cues and prompts—posted rules, steps for performing tasks, etc. • Allowing students to use resources in the environment to recall information—notes, textbooks, pictures, etc. • Relating information to student's previous experiences • Having students outline, highlight, underline, or summarize information that should be remembered • Telling students what to listen for when being given directions or receiving information • Associative cues or mnemonic devices • Teaching visual imagery	• Using only one modality, such as a lecture, to teach a lesson • Expecting students to recall facts without support • Expecting students to utilize mnemonics, visual imagery, technology, or other supports without teaching them how to use these tools

What Works/What Doesn't Work Charts, continued

Area of Concern	What Works	What Doesn't Work
Handwriting	• Focusing on form • Mechanical pencils or grips • Appropriate handwriting program • Assistive technology	• Lengthy handwriting tasks that result in fatigue • Expectations that disregard students' physical weaknesses or limitations
Evaluations and Assessments	• Student/teacher collaboration on the evaluation and assessment methods and tools • Evaluations based on instruction reflecting the key concepts and basic understandings of the curriculum • Providing objectives, study guides, vocabulary, acceptable responses, support, and clarification for questions • Differentiation • Audiotape responses • Graphic organizers in lieu of paragraph responses • Creating a model • Giving a speech	• Lengthy essays • Penalties for spelling in content areas • Time limits • Matching tasks

Note. Adapted fom unpublished charts by Larry March and Martha Abolins. Reprinted with permission.

Bordering on Excellence Tools

The Bordering on Excellence tools drive theory to practice by combining the best practices and guiding principles for appropriate adaptations and accommodations with successful strategies to help teachers tailor instruction for each student. They interface with any instructional material and will allow educators to consider the multiple issues that they need to effectively and efficiently address when differentiating content, process, and product.

The components are:

- *Frame of Reference:* This is a desk and/or notebook reference companion designed to address the differentiated needs and expertise of staff. It is useful for training and teacher/parent conferences. It includes three sections: The Big Picture, Possible Stumbling Blocks, and Adaptations and Accommodations for Overcoming Obstacles. Simply reproduce or copy the pages that follow into a format that suits you best, whether it is several two-sided cards or a packet of information.

- *Bordering on Excellence Frame:* This is a blank frame that provides an alternative format for analyzing either the needs of specific students or evaluating the obstacles inherent in a lesson. It is useful for training and parent/teacher conferences. We have provided examples for you to follow, along with blank frames for each of the four trouble areas faced by smart kids with learning difficulties. These frames can also be used to evaluate instructional materials, including curricular guides, books, teacher-made study guides, and workbooks.

TIPS

Teacher

Use the collection of tools as references, for planning purposes, as a student record form, with instructional materials to obviate student weaknesses and tap into strengths, and as a communication tool with parents, other staff members, and students.

Parent

Use with your child and his teacher when solving homework issues. Use as a basis for discussion at teacher conferences and meetings.

Student

Keep in your notebook as a reference. Work with your teacher and parents to ease difficulties with materials.

Bordering on Excellence Tools

The Big Picture

ENSURE
- Focus on strengths and interests
- Instructional adaptations and accommodations
- Comprehensive case management

TEACH
- Decoding skills
- Writing process
- Language conventions (e.g, spelling, grammar, punctuation, usage)
- Note taking
- Highlighting
- Outlining
- Summarizing
- Prioritizing tasks
- Organizing materials
- Keyboarding
- Word processing

PROVIDE
- Acceleration and enrichment
- Open-ended tasks
- Real-life applications
- Realistic simulations
- Emphasis on problem solving, reasoning, and critical thinking
- Opportunities for student choice
- Alternative product options
- Integration of the arts
- Approach that teaches to various learning styles
- Opportunities to create authentic products
- Multisensory approach to learning
- Flexibility in classroom organization

Bordering on Excellence Tools, continued

Possible Stumbling Blocks

WRITING

- the physical act of putting words on paper
- handwriting
- generating topics
- combining words into meaningful sentences
- organizing sentences and incorporating adequate details and support statements into organized paragraphs
- revising and editing
- using language mechanics effectively (e.g., grammar, punctuation, spelling)

ORGANIZATION

- following multistep directions
- planning the steps needed to complete a task
- organizing desk, locker, notebook, and other materials
- locating needed materials
- breaking long-range assignments into manageable steps
- prioritizing

READING

- decoding unfamiliar words
- inferring meaning of new words
- summarizing
- reading fluently and quickly
- using textbooks

MEMORY

- concentrating and keeping track of information
- quickly recalling details
- retrieving details after time has passed

Bordering on Excellence Tools, continued

Adaptations and Accommodations—Writing

ASSISTIVE TECHNOLOGY	INSTRUCTION MATERIALS	TEACHING/ASSESSMENT	INSTRUCT STUDENTS IN:
• voice recognition software • writing organizational software • electronic spellers and dictionaries • computer with spelling and grammar checker • portable keyboards • word prediction software • programs that read writing aloud, providing for audio spell checker, proofreading, word prediction, and homophone distinction • tape recorder for transcription after student dictation	• step-by-step written directions • a proofreading checklist • graphic organizers • scoring rubric, models, and anchor papers for students to evaluate work • guides such as story starters, webs, and outlines • dictionaries, word banks, and thesauri • personal dictionaries of misused and misspelled words • highlighters to indicate errors and corrections • copy of teacher's notes or of another student's notes (NCR paper) • pencil grips and mechanical pencils • paper with raised lines • slant boards	• focus on content rather than mechanics • focus on quality rather than quantity • prepare storyboards, guided imagery, dramatization, or projects before the writing process • set important purposes for writing, such as writing for publication • allow students to write in areas of interest or expertise • allow students to show understanding through alternative products • reduce or alter written requirements • break down assignments into smaller, manageable parts • allow additional time • proofread for one type of error at a time	• the writing process • prewriting strategies, including brainstorming, making a web, and drawing about the topic • rewriting questions into answer form • writing for a variety of purposes • combining words into meaningful sentences • formulating topic sentences • organizing sentences and incorporating adequate details and support statements into paragraphs • language conventions (e.g., grammar, punctuation, spelling, usage) • history/structure of language • keyboarding skills

Bordering on Excellence Tools, continued

Adaptations and Accommodations—Writing

ASSISTIVE TECHNOLOGY	INSTRUCTION MATERIALS	TEACHING/ASSESSMENT	INSTRUCT STUDENTS IN:
		• permit work with partners or small groups during revising, editing, and proofreading • permit students to use words or phrases instead of complete sentences • allow students to make artistic (visual, spatial, and performing) products • allow students to make scientific and technological products • provide dictated response • students review and summarize important information and directions • invite student questions regarding directions and assignments • provide a portfolio assessment of products and performances • allow alternative spelling • provide students with a list of needed materials and their locations	

Bordering on Excellence Tools, continued

Adaptations and Accommodations—Organization

ASSISTIVE TECHNOLOGY	INSTRUCTION MATERIALS	TEACHING/ASSESSMENT	INSTRUCT STUDENTS IN:
• electronic organizers • software organization programs • audiotaping assignments • e-mailing assignments from school to student's home account	• visual models, storyboards, Venn diagrams, matrices, and flow charts • study guides that help locate information and answers • highlighters, index tabs, and colored stickers • assignment books and calendars for recording assignments • outlines, webs, diagrams, and other graphic organizers	• use short, simple directions • provide advanced organizers regarding what students will know by the end of the lesson • post class and homework assignments in the same area each day and assure that students record them and/or have a printed copy • verbally review class and homework assignments • list and verbally review step-by-step directions for assignments • work with students to establish specific due dates for short assignments and time frames for long-term assignments • break up tasks into workable and obtainable steps • encourage study buddies • give examples and specific steps to accomplish tasks	• how to prioritize tasks • how to ask questions regarding unclear directions and assignments • metacognition • how to break long-term assignments into manageable components • note taking • a routine to follow to prepare for each class • a system for organizing notebooks and lockers • how to use software organization programs • how to use assignment books, calendars, electronic organizers, visual models, and graphic organizers • how to access homework help

Bordering on Excellence Tools, continued

Adaptations and Accommodations—Organization

ASSISTIVE TECHNOLOGY	INSTRUCTION MATERIALS	TEACHING/ASSESSMENT	INSTRUCT STUDENTS IN:
		• provide checkpoints for long-term assignments and monitor progress frequently • students review and summarize important information and directions • invite student questions regarding directions and assignments • provide students with a list of needed materials and their locations • periodically check notebooks and lockers • provide homework hotline or structured homework assistance • post a daily routine and explain any changes in that routine • provide an uncluttered work area • label and store materials in designated locations • provide a specific location for students to place completed work • provide samples of finished products	

Bordering on Excellence Tools, continued

Adaptations and Accommodations—Reading

ASSISTIVE TECHNOLOGY	INSTRUCTION MATERIALS	TEACHING/ASSESSMENT	INSTRUCT STUDENTS IN:
• CD-ROMs with audio component • electronic spellers that speak words aloud • books on tape and digital books • computer programs that allow words to be read aloud • text-to-speech software	• interviews, speakers, and demonstrations • multimedia presentations • tape recorded directions or tests • text study guides and graphic organizers to help locate information • access to challenging reading programs, like Junior Great Books • high-interest, appropriate-level reading material and multilevel texts about the same topic • above-grade-level high-interest reading material • rich literature experiences • expository reading experiences • visuals (outlines, graphic organizers, charts, photographs, diagrams, and maps) to help students understand written information • word banks	• develop interest and curiosity by activating prior knowledge • use a multiple intelligence approach • begin with an experience or project • teach through the arts (drama, visual arts, poetry) • utilize simulations and moral dilemmas • encourage reading related to students' areas of interest • set purposes for reading and state what students should know after reading the text • ask lower level comprehension questions in order to build up to higher level questions • cue students to important words and concepts verbally and through highlighting • teach vocabulary in context	• phonological awareness and phonics • a multisensory reading approach • a rule-based approach to reading • sight vocabulary • prefixes and suffixes • how to use a textbook (i.e., understanding the index, table of contents, glossary, charts, tables, captions, and bold text) • outlining and note taking

Bordering on Excellence Tools, continued

Adaptations and Accommodations—Reading

ASSISTIVE TECHNOLOGY	INSTRUCTION MATERIALS	TEACHING/ASSESSMENT	INSTRUCT STUDENTS IN:
		• give students the opportunity to read silently before reading aloud • allow students to choose whether or not to read aloud • pair students who have strong decoding skills with weak decoders • allow students to do difficult tasks in small groups • read directions or tests aloud • allow additional time for reading • teach students to outline, underline, or highlight important points • encourage students to take notes while reading • offer support and clarification for imbedded directions in text	

Bordering on Excellence Tools, continued

Adaptations and Accommodations—Memory

ASSISTIVE TECHNOLOGY	INSTRUCTION MATERIALS	TEACHING/ASSESSMENT	INSTRUCT STUDENTS IN:
• software programs as an alternative way of presenting information • tape recording directions or information • software programs to organize key points	• multiple modalities when presenting directions, explanations, and instructional content • those that address multiple learning styles • utilize materials that are meaningful to students • copies of the information that highlight key facts	• have students repeat the directions or information back to teacher • have students repeat information to selves • have students recall important details at the end of a lesson • have students sequence activities after a lesson or event • have students teach information to other students • have students deliver the schedule of events to other students • deliver directions, explanations, and instructional content in a clear manner and at an appropriate pace • provide students with a written list of materials and directions • give auditory and visual cues to help students recall information	• transforming information from one modality to another (e.g., from verbal to a diagram or from visual to verbal) • questioning any directions, explanations, and instructions they do not understand • delivering increasingly long verbal messages • how to organize information into smaller units • using environmental sources in the environment to recall information (e.g., notes, pictures) • how to practice memory skills by engaging in activities that are purposeful, such as delivering messages or being in charge of a task • how to highlight and summarize information

Bordering on Excellence Tools, continued

Adaptations and Accommodations—Memory

ASSISTIVE TECHNOLOGY	INSTRUCTION MATERIALS	TEACHING/ASSESSMENT	INSTRUCT STUDENTS IN:
		• provide students with environmental cues and prompts such as posted rules and steps for performing tasks • have students use resources in the environment to recall information (e.g., notes, textbooks, pictures, etc.) • relate information presented to students' previous experiences • have students outline, highlight, underline, or summarize information that should be remembered • repeat information by using different experiences and modalities • provide students with information from a variety of sources • use visual imagery • tell students what to listen for when receiving information	• practicing repetition of information • engaging in memory games and activities • listening skills • visual imagery • systematic ways to store and retrieve information • how to use advanced organizers, such as lists, tables, and graphics • study and test-taking skills • routines for beginning a task • how to recognize key words

Bordering on Excellence Frame Example

Adaptations/Accommodations
WRITING
Possible Stumbling Blocks

- the physical act of putting words on paper
- handwriting
- generating topics
- formulating topic sentences

- combining words into meaningful sentences
- using language mechanics effectively (e.g., grammar, punctuation, spelling)

- organizing sentences and in-corporating adequate details and support statements into organized paragraphs
- revising and editing

Instructional Materials	NOTES:	Teaching/Assessment Methods
<ul><li>step-by-step written directions</li><li>a proofreading checklist</li><li>scoring rubrics, models, and anchor papers for students to evaluate their own work</li><li>graphic organizers</li><li>guides such as story starters, webs, story charts, outlines</li><li>dictionaries, word banks, and thesauri</li><li>personal dictionaries of misused and misspelled words</li><li>highlighter to indicate errors/corrections</li><li>copy of teacher notes or of another student's notes (NCR paper)</li><li>pencil grips</li><li>paper with raised lines</li><li>mechanical pencils</li><li>slant board</li></ul>	*-5 students with difficulties in writing* *-written production required* *· literature webs (2 chapters)* *· vocabulary webs (2 words)* *· change matrix with specific evidence* *· written reflections* *-I will need to address the following:* *· stumbling blocks (circled)* *· interventions (circled)* *· technology (circled)* *-make sure students have access to computers/software* *-concerned with Johnny* *· great ideas, but poor production* *· doesn't have good computer skills* *· needs to be able to dictate ideas on tape or to an adult for transcription* *· needs to be able to use computer with word-predictive software*	<ul><li>focus on content rather than mechanics</li><li>focus on quality rather than quantity</li><li>begin with storyboards, guided imagery, dramatization, or projects before the writing process</li><li>set important purposes for writing, such as writing for publication, writing to an expert, or writing to a famous person</li><li>allow students to write in area of interest or expertise</li><li>allow students to demonstrate understanding through alternative methods/products</li><li>reduce or alter written requirements</li><li>break down assignments into smaller, manageable parts</li><li>additional time</li><li>work with partners or small groups to confer for revising, editing, and proofreading</li></ul>

Assistive Technology

- voice recognition software
- organizational software
- electronic spellers and dictionaries
- tape recorder for student dictation and then transcription

- computer word processor with spelling and grammar checker or talking word processor
- portable keyboards
- word prediction software

- programs that allow writing to be read aloud
- programs that provide for audio spell checker, word prediction, and homophone distinction

Adaptations/Accommodations
READING
Possible Stumbling Blocks

- decoding unfamiliar words
- inferring meaning of new words
- summarizing
- reading fluently and quickly
- using textbooks

Instructional Materials	NOVEL ASSIGNMENT:	Teaching/Assessment Methods

• interviews, guest speakers, and demonstrations
• multimedia presentations
• tape recorded directions or tests
• text study guides and graphic organizers to help students locate information
• above-grade-level high-interest reading material
• high-interest, appropriate-level reading material
	– All students read The Secret Garden by Frances Hodgson Burnett.
	– Students choose one other novel:
	  – Year of Impossible Goodbyes by Sook Nyul Choi
	  – Underrunners by Margaret Mahy
	  – Words by Heart by Ouida Sebestyen
	  – Taking Sides by Gary Soto
	  – Call It Courage by Armstrong Sperry
	– Activities
	(A) Literature Webs for two chapters of each novel.
	(B) List of vocabulary words. Vocabulary Webs for at least two words in each novel.
	(C) Change Matrix with specific evidence for each novel.
		• develop interest and curiosity by activating prior knowledge before reading
		• teach through the arts (drama, visual arts, poetry)
		• encourage reading related to students' areas of interest
		• ask lower level comprehension questions in order to build up to higher level questions
		• teach vocabulary in context
		• allow students to choose whether or not to read aloud
		• allow students to do vocabulary webs, literature webs, and other difficult tasks in small groups
		• teach students to outline, underline, or highlight important points in reading

Note. Taken from *Literary Reflections: Language Arts Unit for High-Ability Learners. Novel Assignment, Handout 3B* by the College of William and Mary Center for Gifted Education, 1998, p. 51. Copyright© 1998 by Kendall/Hunt Publishing.

Assistive Technology

- CD-ROMs with audio component
- electronic spellers that speak words aloud
- books on tape and digital books
- computer programs that allow words to be read aloud
- text-to-speech software

Adaptations/Accommodations
WRITING
Possible Stumbling Blocks

- the physical act of putting words on paper
- handwriting
- generating topics
- formulating topic sentences

- combining words into meaningful sentences
- using language mechanics effectively (e.g., grammar, punctuation, spelling)

- organizing sentences and incorporating adequate details and support statements into organized paragraphs
- revising and editing

Instructional Materials	NOTES:	Teaching/Assessment Methods
• step-by-step written directions • a proofreading checklist • scoring rubrics, models, and anchor papers for students to evaluate their own work • graphic organizers • guides such as story starters, webs, story charts, outlines • dictionaries, word banks, and thesauri • personal dictionaries of misused and misspelled words • highlighter to indicate errors/corrections • copy of teacher notes or of another student's notes (NCR paper) • pencil grips • paper with raised lines • mechanical pencils • slant board		• focus on content rather than mechanics • focus on quality rather than quantity • begin with storyboards, guided imagery, dramatization, or projects before the writing process • set important purposes for writing, such as writing for publication, writing to an expert, or writing to a famous person • allow students to write in area of interest or expertise • allow students to demonstrate understanding through alternative methods/products • reduce or alter written requirements • break down assignments into smaller, manageable parts • additional time • work with partners or small groups to confer for revising, editing, and proofreading

Assistive Technology

- voice recognition software
- organizational software
- electronic spellers and dictionaries
- tape recorder for student dictation and then transcription

- computer word processor with spelling and grammar checker or talking word processor
- portable keyboards
- word prediction software

- programs that allow writing to be read aloud
- programs that provide for audio spell checker, word prediction, and homophone distinction

Adaptations/Accommodations

READING

Possible Stumbling Blocks

- decoding unfamiliar words
- inferring meaning of new words
- summarizing
- reading fluently and quickly
- using textbooks

Instructional Materials	NOTES:	Teaching/Assessment Methods
• interviews, guest speakers, and demonstrations • multimedia presentations • tape recorded directions or tests • text study guides and graphic organizers to help students locate information • above-grade-level high-interest reading material • high-interest, appropriate-level reading material		• develop interest and curiosity by activating prior knowledge before reading • teach through the arts (drama, visual arts, poetry) • encourage reading related to students' areas of interest • ask lower level comprehension questions in order to build up to higher level questions • teach vocabulary in context • allow students to choose whether or not to read aloud • allow students to do vocabulary webs, literature webs, and other difficult tasks in small groups • teach students to outline, underline, or highlight important points in reading

Assistive Technology

- CD-ROMs with audio component
- electronic spellers that speak words aloud
- books on tape and digital books
- computer programs that allow words to be read aloud
- text-to-speech software

Adaptations/Accommodations

ORGANIZATION

Possible Stumbling Blocks

- following multistep directions
- planning the steps needed to complete a task
- organizing desk, locker, notebook, and other materials
- locating needed materials
- breaking long-range assignments into manageable steps
- prioritizing

Instructional Materials	NOTES:	Teaching/Assessment Methods
• visual models, storyboards, Venn diagrams, matrices, and flow charts • study guides that assist with locating information and answers • highlighters, index tabs, and colored stickers • assignment books and calendars for recording assignments • outlines, webs, diagrams, and other graphic organizers		• use short, simple directions • post class and homework assignments in the same area each day and assure that students record them and/or have a printed copy • verbally review class and homework assignments • work with students to establish specific due dates for short assignments and time frames for long-term assignments • break up tasks into workable and obtainable steps • provide checkpoints for long-term assignments and monitor progress frequently • provide homework hotline or structured homework assistance • provide a specific location for students to place completed work

Assistive Technology

- electronic organizers
- software organization programs
- audiotaping assignments
- e-mailing assignments from school to student's home account

Adaptations/Accommodations

MEMORY

Possible Stumbling Blocks

- concentrating and keeping track of information
- quickly recalling details
- retrieving details after time has passed

Instructional Materials	NOTES:	Teaching/Assessment Methods
• use multiple modalities when presenting directions, explanations, and instructional content • provide students with copies of the information that highlight key facts • use materials that are meaningful to students • address multiple learning styles		• have students repeat the directions or information back to teacher • have students recall important details at the end of a lesson or period of time • have students teach information to other students • deliver directions, explanations, and instructional content clearly • provide students with environmental cues and prompts such as posted rules and steps for performing tasks • provide students with written list of materials and directions • give auditory and visual cues to help students to recall information • provide adequate opportunities for repetition of information through different experiences and modalities

Assistive Technology

- teachers use software programs as an alternative or additional way of presenting information
- students tape record directions or information
- students use software programs for organization of key points

Differentiation Checklist

Differentiating instruction is imperative for planning and implementing instruction in order to meet the diverse needs of twice-exceptional students. The careful analysis of students' strengths, challenges, and learning styles will aid in designing appropriate opportunities, resources, and activities for students to show what they know.

TIPS

Teacher

Use this checklist to plan for implementing differentiation in your classroom. Use it as an evaluation tool to ascertain whether you do implement differentiation. Share with parents as an indicator of the differentiation practices in your classroom and how it is utilized for their child.

Parent

Use this checklist as an evaluation tool to ascertain whether differentiation is implemented in your child's class.

Differentiation Checklist

Directions: Use the following checklist as you plan and implement differentiation within your classroom. This is not a complete list, but rather a starting point.

_____ Use a variety of assessments to discover what students know, including test data, pretests, writing samples, discussions, observations, products, and parent and student input.

_____ Provide positive expectations and respect for individual differences.

_____ Support strength-based instruction in content, process, and product.

_____ Provide for acceleration and enrichment.

_____ Provide appropriate adaptations and accommodations.

_____ Integrate basic skills and higher level questioning and thinking in the curriculum.

_____ Provide opportunities for critical and creative thinking.

_____ Provide a variety of classroom resources and materials with several levels of difficulty.

_____ Provide flexible grouping.

_____ Provide for guided and independent work.

_____ Offer a variety of activities and allow for student choice.

_____ Provide for alternative products to allow students to show what they know.

_____ Allow students to make decisions about creating and presenting original topics.

_____ Use a variety of assistive technology tools.

_____ Help students monitor and evaluate their own work.

_____ Use varied, stimulating, and performance-based assessments.

Note. Reprinted from _101 School Success Tools for Smart Kids With Learning Difficulties_ (p. 93) by B. Roffman Shevitz, M. Stemple, L. Barnes-Robinson, and S. Jeweler, 2011, New York, NY: Taylor & Francis. Copyright 2011 Taylor & Francis. Reprinted with permission.

Differentiation Pyramid

The pyramid is a conceptual look at differentiating activities within the classroom. You can record content, process, or product ideas. Use the blank template as you plan for the students in your class.

TIPS

Teacher

Use the pyramid template as an aid that illustrates what you want the students to be able to know, understand and be able to do. Decide how you are going to differentiate: readiness, interests, learning profiles, and content, process, and product.

Parent

The pyramid is designed to help you visualize the concept of differentiated instruction in the classroom. You will note that the learning goal is the same for all students, while the activity to arrive at the understanding may be different.

Student

Look at the sample pyramid. Based on your interest in the topic and the type of activity offered, where do you see yourself fitting best? Would it change, depending on the topic? Think about a topic that you are interested in and design an activity that would be of interest to you.

Differentiation Pyramid

Directions: The pyramid is a conceptual look at differentiating activities within the classroom. You can record content, process, or product ideas. Use the blank template as you plan for the students in your class.

Activities Involving a Few Students:
I will work with a mentor to learn how to construct a scale model of a Medieval building.

Activities Involving Some Students:
We want to learn about vaulted ceilings so we can construct a Medieval cathedral.

Activities Involving Many, But Not All Students:
Let's make models of buildings that existed during the Middle Ages.

Activities Involving All Students:
We are studying the Middle Ages, so everyone will watch a video on castles and cathedrals.

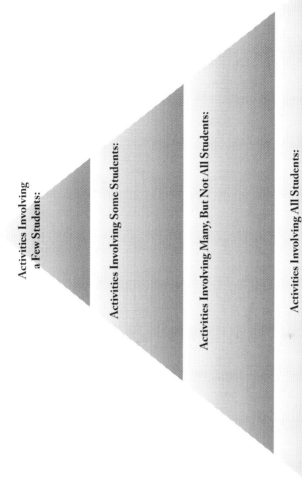

Activities Involving a Few Students:

Activities Involving Some Students:

Activities Involving Many, But Not All Students:

Activities Involving All Students:

Note. Reprinted from *101 School Success Tools for Smart Kids With Learning Difficulties* (p. 193–194) by B. Roffman Shevitz, M. Stemple, L. Barnes-Robinson, and S. Jeweler, 2011, New York, NY: Taylor & Francis. Copyright 2011 Taylor & Francis. Reprinted with permission.

Assistive Technology

Bright students with learning difficulties love technology! Many are naturally drawn to video games, computers, and the latest gadgets; they love to use them and think about how they work. Tap into this inherent interest by using technology in the classroom for instruction and teaching them how to use assistive technology (AT) designed to assist students with disabilities. Today's 21st-century teachers use a variety of technologies for instruction such as PowerPoint-assisted lectures, streaming video clips, WebQuests, pictures from Google Images, Promethean Boards, and more. Struggling readers can use a variety of tools and software (e.g., MP3 players, Kurzweil 3000, Write:OutLoud, ReadPlease, WordQ) to listen to text that is above their reading level. Struggling writers benefit from software (e.g., Inspiration, WordQ, Clicker, Write:OutLoud, Draft:Builder, Dragon NaturallySpeaking, SpeakQ) to support their organizational, spelling, handwriting, and note-taking difficulties. Students are more engaged when teachers use technology as part of the process of learning. Using technology allows students to move from dependence to independence.

TIPS

Teacher

Review the software included in the chart. Familiarize yourself with those that you may not have had a chance to use.

Parent

Use the chart when looking at the student characteristics and decide what matches your child the best. Review the software that is suggested for the child with those characteristics. Make a point of investigating any of the software listed that you are unfamiliar with to see if it may be an effective tool for your child.

Student

How many of the software materials listed in the chart are you familiar with? Think about what types of things make it difficult for you to learn. Looking at the software capabilities, do you see any software that may be helpful for you to have? Talk to your teacher to see if the school already has access to those that sound interesting. Talk to your parents about the option to invest in any for use at home.

Assistive Technology

Directions: Consider the needs of your student as you plan for his success within a lesson or unit. Select tools that will level the playing field and allow the student to fully access information and demonstrate knowledge.

Student Characteristics	Software Capabilities	Software to Consider
Strong listening comprehension; poor decoding, reading fluency, study, and writing skills.	Scanning/reading software reads text aloud to the student. Study and writing tools sometimes are also embedded.	Screen readers (e.g., Kurzweil 3000, ReadPlease, NaturalReader)
Strong vocabulary and knows what he wants to say, but has poor spelling skills.	Word prediction provides word choices for the student to select from based on initial letters typed. Will read options to student.	Word prediction (e.g., Co:Writer, WordQ)
Has lots of ideas but lacks organization of ideas; does not fully develop details and support for his ideas; ideas and vocabulary are strong but memory and spelling are poor.	Prewriting/organization allows the student to create or complete graphic organizers, outlines, and/or word banks.	Prewriting software (e.g., Kidspiration, Inspiration, Clicker)
Poor fine motor skills; reluctant writer.	Word processing supports writing composition, revising, and editing.	Word processing (e.g., Microsoft Word)
Strong verbal skills but struggles with writing; can't reflect the full extent of his knowledge on paper.	Voice recognition allows the student to dictate ideas verbally into a microphone and the student's words will appear on the computer screen.	Voice recognition (e.g., Dragon Dictation, SpeakQ)
Strong math reasoning and problem solving; lacks automaticity or recall of math facts.	Calculation device supports math calculation.	Calculator

Note. Reprinted from *101 School Success Tools for Smart Kids With Learning Difficulties* (pp. 130–131, 196) by B. Roffman Shevitz, M. Stemple, L. Barnes-Robinson, and S. Jeweler, 2011, New York, NY: Taylor & Francis. Copyright 2011 Taylor & Francis. Reprinted with permission.

Academic ORR

This chart illustrates how the ORR model can be used when analyzing a student in the academic areas.

Academic ORR

Observe	Reflect	Respond
Reads slowly and has weak decoding skills, thus he does not comprehend text read independently.	• Has the student received systematic instruction in phonemic awareness and phonics? • Is he making progress?	• Provide systematic/decoding reading instruction and collect progress data frequently.
Listens raptly during read-alouds and participates orally in discussions about text, making inferences and connections easily.	• Is the student's listening comprehension ability significantly stronger than his basic reading ability?	• Include the student in high-level reading groups with appropriate supports (e.g., recorded books, read-alouds).
Writes with nonphonetic spelling. Written vocabulary use does not match with oral vocabulary sophistication.	• Does the student lack phonemic awareness and sound-symbol association required for phonetic spelling?	• Provide systematic decoding/encoding instruction.
Writes minimally with little elaboration, support, or detail despite ability to share orally at length and in great detail.	• Does the student have executive functioning or organizational challenges that are interfering with his ability to express his ideas in writing?	• Provide instruction in strategies for developing and organizing ideas prior to writing (e.g., graphic organizers, outlines, lists). • Take dictation or provide verbal preconference.
Makes frequent errors in math calculation and lacks automatic recall of basic math facts despite having advanced math-reasoning ability.	• Does the student's difficulty interfere with his ability to solve higher level math problems? • Does the student have the number sense but lack the memory for the facts?	• Provide a calculator or reference sheet to support calculations (e.g., multiplication table) during math problem-solving tasks.
Great in science but has difficulty completing the steps of experiments.	• Does the student have difficulty following multistep directions?	• Partner with a student with strong organizational skills. • Provide written checklists.

Observe	Reflect	Respond
Great ideas for a project but lacks follow-through and doesn't get it done.	• Does the student have difficulty planning and executing long-term tasks?	• Break down the task into smaller parts. • Frequently check the student's progress on the project.

Note. Reprinted from *101 School Success Tools for Smart Kids With Learning Difficulties* (p. 64) by B. Roffman Shevitz, M. Stemple, L. Barnes-Robinson, and S. Jeweler, 2011, New York, NY: Taylor & Francis. Copyright 2011 Taylor & Francis. Reprinted with permission.

Who's Who: Roles and Responsibilities

The list that follows gives a brief synopsis of the roles and responsibilities of the professionals who may be involved in the lives of GT/LD students.

TIPS

Teacher

Use as a resource of roles and responsibilities in your school and school system.

Parent

Use as a resource of the different roles and responsibilities of staff in your school and school system.

Student

Understand the roles and identify the people in your school who can help you.

Who's Who: Roles and Responsibilities

Teacher Advisor/Case Manager (point of entry contact): Monitors students' overall progress, contacts parents regularly about progress, administers triennial reevaluations, develops IEPs, consults with classroom teachers, solves problems, and refers unresolved issues to appropriate staff.

General Education Teachers: Collaborate with special educators, instruct students in curricula, and provide accommodations and modifications.

Special Education Teachers: Ensure access to challenging and rigorous curricula, work on relevant IEP goals, accommodate and modify lessons, individually plan for and evaluate student progress, and instruct students in strategies and skills necessary to access curriculum.

Related Service Providers (Speech Language Pathologists, Occupational Therapists, Physical Therapists, etc.): Provide related services, administer evaluations, evaluate progress, develop IEPs, and support classroom teachers.

Special Education Instructional Assistants (SEIA): Support classroom instruction, provide accommodations and modifications for students, teach small-group lessons, and assist teachers in any way necessary to ensure a well-run classroom environment.

Elementary and Secondary School Counselors: Schedule and counsel all students and provide information on resources; usually occurs on the middle and high school level.

Resource Teacher for Special Education (RTSE): Coordinates special education services and collaborates with and supports GT/LD coordinators, administration, educators, parents, and students.

GT/LD Instructional Specialist: Oversees GT/LD programs, helps identify and place new students, trains staff, and serves as a resource for information on GT/LD education.

Administration (Principal, Vice Principal, Student Support Specialist, etc.): Oversee schoolwide issues, monitor programs, provide instructional leadership, and serve as resources for coordinators and parents.

Consultant: An individual, independent from the school system, who provides expertise in facilitating appropriate intervention and placement decisions.

4

WHAT DO GOOD PROGRAMS AND SERVICES LOOK LIKE?

Programs and services for smart kids with learning difficulties must respond to a range of needs and abilities. These services need to be developed in all grades and be clearly defined and articulated for parents, students, and school staff. Students need opportunities to learn at an accelerated pace, with great depth and breadth. As educators and parents, we must find a way of unleashing the potential and freeing the power within all of our children regardless of gender, race, cultural background, or socioeconomic levels, in order to discover their interests and develop their strengths. Parents, the information here should be used as a guide to choosing and evaluating the accommodations your student receives. In addition, you may want to share this information with your child's school.

 DOI:10.4324/9781003237983-5

Student programming should include challenging instruction, flexible grouping, and schedules that enable students to spend time with their intellectual peers for in-depth study in all subject areas. In the elementary years, opportunities for cluster groupings of bright students need to be created within individual classrooms or grade levels, and if needed, across grade levels. Cluster groupings are groups of four to eight students at a similar instructional level. In the middle school years, gifted or advanced classes are good options for GT students with disabilities, as well as cluster grouping in all subject areas. When students reach high school, there should be opportunities for them to take honors and Advanced Placement or International Baccalaureate courses in all of the major disciplines and in many of the electives offered.

There are special programs at all levels in many districts for those few students needing something very different and more intense. Opportunities might include gifted and talented elementary centers (self-contained classes of highly gifted students), gifted/LD centers (a small class in a special education setting for students identified as both gifted and disabled), magnet centers (programs with an interdisciplinary curriculum focus in particular disciplines), and International Baccalaureate (IB) programs. In 1965, the International Baccalaureate Organization (IBO) established a program of studies to ensure high-quality educational standards for students studying in international schools throughout the world. The IBO offers an internationally recognized diploma based on in-depth study of major content areas.

Students should be encouraged to try the advanced courses and programs at all levels if they demonstrate the motivation for advanced studies and/or have the prerequisites needed. Students with learning challenges may need the support of special education providers, counselors, and other specialists to be successful in more rigorous and challenging classes. For some students, the appropriate accommodations and adaptations will be the key to their success. Under no circumstances should students with unique needs and strengths be excluded from these opportunities.

OPTIONS FOR THE EDUCATION OF BRIGHT STUDENTS WITH LEARNING DIFFICULTIES

Many public school systems and private schools have put in place a consultative program to meet the needs of bright students with learning challenges. A specialist with expertise in the education of these students helps the other school staff, particularly the classroom teachers, to utilize the best practices in providing appropriate education. Schools and school systems without identified specialists should designate someone to perform this role. Typically a GT teacher, special educator, counselor, or administrator will take on leadership in this area. The following task analysis illustrates the process that these specialists undertake as they create rigorous and supportive programs for their bright underachieving students:

- Analyze what the roles and responsibilities of the educators are within the school.
- Assign the roles and responsibilities to the educators within the school.
- Set up a collaborative climate. Team planning facilitates inclusion of these students in the regular classroom.
- Collect and study data related to the students (e.g., test scores, performance in school, performance in the community).
- Extend each child's intellectual boundaries and help all students achieve their highest potential.
- Identify all students who have the capability, motivation, or potential to accept the challenge of taking honors, AP, IB, and advanced-level courses, and provide them with the opportunity to do so.
- Focus on students' strengths and interests. Ensure that differentiated educational programs and/or services are systematically provided for bright students in all grades, including students with learning disabilities or other special needs.
- Provide accelerated and enriched instruction, including appropriate strategy and skill instruction and instructional adaptations and accommodations while imple-

menting students' IEPs, 504 plans, or other less formal plans.

- Analyze curricula to identify key concepts.
- Collect resources and materials (e.g., curricular guides, programs, software).
- Choose appropriate resources, materials, strategies, and techniques.
- Plan for alternative learning activities.
- Plan units and lessons.
- Collect appropriate adaptations and accommodations for each student.
- Implement units and lessons.
- Plan for assessments that capitalize on students' strengths and work around their weaknesses.
- Evaluate successful/best practices.
- Schedule team meetings to discuss students. Specific weekly, bimonthly, or monthly meeting times allow for ongoing planning and an opportunity to discuss and evaluate student progress. Difficulties are addressed before they multiply and escalate.
- Know and understand the social-emotional profile of each student in order to provide strategies that alleviate frustration and create motivation and interest in school learning.
- Train teachers (possibly during in-service) on working with smart students with learning challenges, including their characteristics, needs, strategies, adaptations, and accommodations.
- Train students and parents on various resources, materials, and strategies.
- Keep lines of communication open between and among staff, students, and parents.

Self-Contained Public School Programs

Few public school programs have had ongoing, comprehensive programs that included special classrooms for meeting the needs of twice-exceptional students. The Montgomery County Public Schools GT/LD program is described in detail below, both as an example of best practices in action and as a guide for parents or school systems that may be interested in developing a similar program (Weinfeld et al., 2002).

The Montgomery County Public Schools (MCPS) program. Determined to address the needs of their gifted and learning disabled students, educators in MCPS have spent many years creating a dynamic, comprehensive program for their gifted and learning disabled student population. In 1986, MCPS initiated a pilot program to explore the incidence rate of students with high cognitive ability that were experiencing learning difficulties (Starnes, Ginevan, Stokes, & Barton, 1988). With initial funding from the Javits grant program, promising developments have occurred in the Montgomery County Public Schools. MCPS identifies gifted students with varying degrees of learning disabilities and has developed special self-contained classes for gifted students with severe learning disabilities while those with moderate and mild disabilities receive services in general education classes (Starnes et al., 1998).

GT/LD students in grades 2–12 receive appropriate instruction, adaptations, and accommodations related to their disability. Successful, practical programming is based on solid research and theory. GT/LD students are guaranteed access to accelerated and enriched instruction that maintains the rigor and high standards expected of all gifted students. As with other gifted students, the range of instructional opportunities available to GT/LD students are provided in gifted classes in elementary and middle school, in honors and Advanced Placement classes at the high school, in highly selective gifted and magnet programs in grades 4–12, and through differentiation in general education classes at all levels. In addition, GT/LD students with severe learning disabilities receive appropriate gifted instruction within GT/LD Center Programs. Gifted underachieving students also have the opportunity to participate in a mentor program designed to nurture their talents and develop their potential. The comprehensiveness of the delivery of GT/LD programming is what makes this one of the unique programs serving this population.

The MCPS model is also unique because it simultaneously addresses the giftedness and the academic needs of each student regardless of his or her grade level or the severity of his or her disability. Overseeing all of the instructional and program opportunities is a full-time program coordinator with expertise in both gifted education and special education. Drawing on the best practices others have researched, and from its teachers' and administrators' own field experiences, MCPS has combined the most successful components of teaching GT/LD students into a strength-based, integrated, and collaborative program.

The following profile is a snapshot of a student-centered classroom with a view into the workings, resources, and climate for students within the MCPS GT/LD Center Programs:

> The room was a buzz of activity. Steven was working on an independent study project at a computer as he listened to a book that had been converted from text to speech. A group of students was sitting and working at a round table with a variety of resource materials related to their in-depth study of whales. Rachel, returning from her social studies mainstream class, began dictating a biographical sketch on Sacagawea into her iPad. Frank was meeting with the teacher at the front table about the next steps in his research project. Student products from their Structures unit lined the bookcases under the windows. The student-made three-dimensional projects reflected concepts learned in both math and science. Junior Great Books, software products, reference materials, large-print books, science equipment, and math equipment filled the shelves. On the walls of the classroom, colorful posters, class standards and expectations, message boards, and plans for the day were displayed. The workstations had a collection of tools that were always available to the students—pens, pencils, tablets, eReaders, tape recorders, graphic organizers, and calculators.

Note that in this classroom, the activity is purposeful and planned, and the interdisciplinary instruction and multiple tools and opportunities for choice are the norm.

The first MCPS Center Program for gifted and learning disabled students opened in 1987 for fourth and fifth graders. Since that time, this program has expanded across the county to its present level of one primary (grades 2–3) and one upper level (grades 4–5) class housed in one elementary school, as well as three middle school programs and three high school programs. The instructional program has focused on developing strengths; providing classroom organization that is flexible and collaborative to maximize goal setting, self-direction, group discussion, self-reflection, problem solving, and self-evaluation; and providing curriculum and instruction that is inquiry-based with a thinking focus.

Although the vast majority of gifted students with learning disabilities in MCPS are served in their home schools with varying degrees of support and accommodations, GT/LD students who are not demonstrating academic progress in their home schools are considered for the GT/LD Center Programs. The GT/LD Center Programs serve students who have both a documented superior cognitive ability and an identified learning disability. The majority of students accepted into the program score two standard deviations above the mean (130) on at least one of the four indices of the WISC-IV, or comparable intelligence scales. Identification of the gift does not rely solely on broad IQ scores. Strong performance on IQ subtests, as well as other less formal evidence of giftedness is considered. Strengths of these students often include superior ability in forming concepts, abstract reasoning, vocabulary, creativity, math reasoning, science, and the arts.

In addition to superior cognitive ability, GT/LD students demonstrate a significant learning disability with academic deficits that are severe enough to drive the need for reduced staff-student ratio and special education supports throughout the day. Learning disabled students, as defined by state regulations, have a deficit in one or more of the basic psychological processes involved in understanding or using language. The deficit affects performance in one or more of the areas of written language, reading, or mathematics. The GT/LD Center Programs serve students who demonstrate academic deficits that are severe enough that barriers to achievement cannot be overcome through accommodations and modifications in the student's home school. These Center Programs provide access to GT instruction for students who would not have access otherwise.

An IEP team considers this placement as part of the school-based periodic or annual IEP review meeting. The school IEP teams refer students who are candidates for this program to their local supervisor of special education. A small committee of individuals who are familiar with the GT/LD program and the characteristics of the students in the program then conduct a review of the candidate. The committee includes the program coordinator for GT/LD programs, a representative from the GT department, and a school psychologist. If a difference of opinion regarding the placement exists, or if there is a need to clarify certain issues, the case is considered by the central IEP team, which then identifies the appropriate placement. The goal is to serve students in their home school, therefore, students placed in the GT/LD Center Program must demonstrate a limited response to their home school's attempt to modify the student's program and provide sufficient interventions over a significant period of time.

At all grade levels in Montgomery County, students in GT/LD Center Programs receive instruction that focuses on developing their strengths and improving existing skills in their areas of weakness. The GT/LD programs are housed in general education school facilities, enabling students to participate with their nondisabled peers wherever possible. Students may enter and exit the program at any grade level. Students typically are mainstreamed for physical education and the arts, as well as lunch and other general activities. They are later mainstreamed in other subject areas as they demonstrate readiness to handle the academic and organizational demands of those subjects. Students typically need special education staff in the classroom with them as they begin their mainstream experiences. As students near the point of exiting the program, they have developed the self-advocacy and compensatory skills necessary to handle the mainstream environment without direct staff support. Middle school and high school students are generally ready for participation in the mainstream. General educators at the secondary level also tend to be specialists in their content areas and, whenever possible, it is beneficial for students to have access to these specialists.

Therefore, the middle school and high school models incorporate more team-teaching situations, giving GT/LD students opportunities to participate in the mainstream classroom with additional support. Similarly, both as a result of having spent several years in the program and because of their developmental maturity, more of the middle and high school students are able to take responsibility for their own accommodations and learning. More students are ready to exit the program at the upper grades than lower grade levels. The elementary GT/LD programs have a greater focus on the teaching and development of skills and compensatory strategies, while the secondary programs have more of a focus on implementing these skills and strategies throughout content areas. At every grade level, the primary focus remains on developing the gifts of these students.

The GT/LD classes are staffed in the same way as other special education programs for students with severe learning disabilities. The teachers are all special education certified and receive ongoing training in the education of gifted and talented students. A full-time program coordinator helps manage all of these programs and provides consultation and training for all staff working with GT/LD students.

Implementation of effective instructional programming for GT/LD students has been a collaborative effort between the district's Division of Accelerated and Enriched Instruction (Gifted and Talented Office) and its Department of Special Education during the last 25 years. This collaboration has provided an opportunity to draw on what are known to be the best practices from both special education and gifted education (Brody & Mills, 1997). The ongoing dialogue and trust between the departments has built a partnership that serves students well.

One elementary school serves as a home to two special GT/LD classrooms. Students typically spend a majority of their academic day in these special classrooms, which are staffed with one special education teacher and one paraeducator. Class sizes vary, but on average there are 8–12 students. The focus of the elementary program is to provide students with instruction in their areas of strength while simultaneously working to improve areas affected by their disabilities. Students become familiar with accommodations, such as computer software programs, that can work around their disabilities. A multisensory approach allows students to utilize and recognize their areas of strength. As students demonstrate proficiency in various subject areas and progress to the point that they can be successful, they may be mainstreamed for part of the day, with appropriate support and accommodations. When mainstreamed, students are included with their nondisabled peers in classes that provide the appropriate rigor and challenge they need.

Each of the three regionally located middle schools serves as a home to students who are GT/LD and who need special education support for a majority of their academic day. Students may be placed in a special education classroom for instruction in their areas of disability. They are typically placed in small classes with other GT/LD students in English and reading, but they are usually placed in the mainstream classroom with their nondisabled gifted peers for social studies and science. A special educator often provides direct support in these classes, sometimes through a team-teaching approach. Depending on the strengths and needs of an individual student, math may be delivered in a self-contained, special education class, a supported mainstream class, or a fully mainstreamed setting. An additional period for providing special education instruction may be offered through the secondary resource room. The resource room may provide instruction in areas addressed in an individual student's IEP, such as learning skills, thinking skills, communication skills, technology skills, and interpersonal skills. Case managers in these GT/LD settings have a smaller than typical staff to student ratio, allowing for more intensive communication with other school staff, as well as with parents. Case managers work with students to help them to understand their unique strengths and needs and to help them to increasingly be able to advocate on their own for accommodations that will allow them access to accelerated and enriched instruction. Students typically spend more and more of their time in mainstream classes during the course of their middle school years.

Most students who have participated in the elementary and/or middle school special GT/LD settings are ready to enter their home high schools or highly gifted magnet programs. There they may receive the support of a secondary resource period(s) and a case manager as they take on the challenge of high school offerings, including honors and/or Advanced Placement courses. Students who need the more intensive support of a special GT/LD setting may be served at one of the three regionally located high schools. Most students who are identified as GT/LD typically are in mainstream classes for the vast majority of their day. Case managers in these settings have a smaller than typical staff to student ratio, allowing for more intensive communication with staff, parents, and students. There is a special education assistive technology center in each of the schools, staffed by a paraeducator throughout the day. Students or their teachers may arrange for students to receive extra accommodations, including the use of word processors, text-to-speech software, speech-to-text software, or special education assistance in this special center at any time during the school day. For a complete updated look at GT/LD programs and services in Maryland's Montgomery County Public Schools, visit the district's website at http://www.montgomeryschoolsmd.org/curriculum/enriched/gtld.

Charter Schools

Charter schools may be alternatives to schools in the public school system. Promising student academic success, charters receive waivers from public schools. However, if the charter school statistics reveal that the school lags behind a comparable public school, the charter can be cancelled and the school closed (Chen, 2007). It is very important for parents to investigate how a charter school addresses the needs of twice-exceptional students before enrolling the child. Check out websites and contact the school with questions and concerns regarding programs and services for twice-exceptional students. For example, the Vida Charter School in Pennsylvania explains on its website (http://vidacharterschool.com) that if a student is determined to be GT/LD, instruction may include the use of project-based learning, Gardner's (1983) multiple intelligences, learning centers, and mentors. Some other examples of charter schools that serve twice-exceptional students are Westgate Community School (http://westgateschool.org), Stargate School (http://stargateschool.org), and the Academy for Advanced and Creative Learning (http://www.academyacl.org), all of which are located in Colorado.

Talent Development Programs

Bright students, especially those with learning challenges, must be provided opportunities that focus on their gifts, enabling them not only to develop a positive self-concept, but also the realization of their potential. Project High Hopes, the Schoolwide Enrichment Model (Renzulli & Reis, 1997), and the Wings Mentor Program, are examples of successful programs that have been developed on this principle.

Project High Hopes, developed by Susan Baum, Carolyn R. Cooper, Terry W. Neu, and Steve Owen (1997), was a curriculum designed to help middle school teachers develop student talents. Student talents were identified and, through authentic problem-solving experiences, the students gained a deep understanding of the principles of science and technology and the visual and performing arts.

The Schoolwide Enrichment Model, developed by Joseph S. Renzulli, consists of activities for individuals and small groups to investigate real-world problems by using appropriate methods of inquiry. Teachers are responsible for helping students focus an area of concern into a solvable problem. The next step is to provide them with the tools necessary to solve the problem and assist them in communicating their results to an authentic audience. Many ready-to-use classroom products focused on the Schoolwide Enrichment Model are available; see http://www.routledge.com to find these tools.

Beginning in 1989, the Wings Mentor Program in the Montgomery County Public Schools was developed to provide additional support to GT/LD students who were not suc-ceeding in the classroom (Shevitz et al., 2003). The goal of this program was to provide students with the opportunity for a successful learning experience by pairing them with mentors who would nurture them, while increasing their knowledge and skills in an area of interest. The program was designed to focus on the students' strengths and their potential for success in order to enhance their self-esteem and self-confidence. The intent of the program was to provide students with the stim-ulation and motivation needed to enable them to begin to be successful in school. The Wings Mentor Program was founded on four basic principles:

- *Focus on strengths.* The focus for gifted underachieving students is on their abilities. In the mentor program, the attention is directed to the students' strengths and interests and their potential for success.
- *Build on success.* The program is designed to maximize student success. By working one-on-one with a mentor in an area of interest, the program provides the students with an opportunity to be successful and gain an aware-ness of their abilities.
- *Enhance self-esteem.* Through their successes, students gain self-confidence, which in turn may contribute to increased self-esteem. A desired outcome is that the students will become excited about school and begin to believe in themselves.
- *Plant a seed.* The intent of the program is to plant seeds for future success. Although the program may not be able to reverse the patterns of underachievement in such a limited time, it may serve as a catalyst for posi-tive change.

Obtaining the right mentors is crucial to the success of the program. In the Wings program, the mentors have a strong education background or have experience working with chil-dren outside of the school environment. They are carefully screened and selected based on their knowledge and their abil-ity to share their skills with young people. Although newly acquired knowledge and the final products the students create are important, the relationship that develops between the mentor and the student is most significant. During weekly meetings, the mentor guides the student in an area of study and provides him or her with needed support. Although they are not counselors, they are trained to be constantly aware of and sensitive to the student's self-concept and to weave self-esteem building strategies into their work where appropriate. It is the mentor-to-student relationship that is a catalyst for improving the students' view of themselves, empowering them to be successful in the classroom.

The mentors meet with their students during the school day for an hour each week for 8 weeks. During these sessions, students explore their selected topics of interest. Some students take this unique time to study an existing area of passion in depth, while others use the time to explore new areas. The students direct their own learning, while acquiring skills in problem solving, planning, goal setting, research, and organization. Most importantly, the mentors help the students learn new strategies and methods to circumvent their weaknesses, allowing them to demonstrate what they have learned in their areas of strength. Over the course of the mentor sessions, students develop and complete a final project that reflects what they have learned. The products are typically hands-on and experiential, enabling the students to gain awareness of their capabilities and learning styles.

Students present their projects to an appropriate audience, usually in their classroom. The final product and presentation are an integral aspect of the program because it not only provides a means of holding the students accountable for their time with the mentor, but more importantly, creates a venue for the students to share their knowledge and experience with classmates. One of the most powerful aspects of the mentor program occurs during the presentation. It is often then that the students' peers and teachers recognize the students' gifts and talents for the first time. In many cases, the success of the project helps to change the student's self-perception. By accentuating the strengths and minimizing the student's areas of weakness, the mentor program increases the student's self-concept and self-esteem.

Marking the culmination of the program is Show-off Night, a special evening when the students come to display their projects, share their experiences, and celebrate their accomplishments. Although the argument can be made that every student could benefit from the unique one-on-one attention that a mentor has to offer, the program is critical to those who are at risk of failing and, yet, possess such great potential. (For more information on the Wings Mentor Program visit http://www.montgomeryschoolsmd.org/curriculum/enriched/gtld.)

One parent's feedback captures the spirit and power of the mentor/student relationship:

Thank you for encouraging our daughter Cecilia to participate in the Wings Mentor Program. Her experience was transformational. Cecilia is a wonderful, bright child who struggles at school, most notably with writing and open-ended projects. We were certain she would choose some type of science project for her creation. Much to our surprise, Cecilia's mentor guided her through a project where she literally wrote 14 chapters of a book. I've never seen Cecilia so proud. And for a child that was always insecure about her writing she has now developed a new confidence believing that not only can she write but that she can write well.

The experience was so valuable because of Cecilia's mentor, Ms. R. She is extraordinary. She was patient, encouraging, and, most important, she allowed Cecilia to really take ownership of her writing. She was able to figure out how Cecilia thinks and to realize that her struggles with writing are often because of the models and formulas she is given—in order to write she needs to process and organize her information and thoughts in a different manner than the way she has been taught in school. This understanding and appreciation of Cecilia's learning style is something that we hope to share with Cecilia's future teachers. I was also incredibly impressed with the relationship Cecilia built with Ms. R, it was a true mentorship and Cecilia walked away having enormous respect and affection for Ms. R.

Private School Options

Fourth- and fifth-grade reading students stand and trace letters in the air, combining aspects of Brain Gym and the Orton-Gillingham reading method. Eighth-grade English students voluntarily come to the front of the class carrying sentence strips, putting their sentence fragments together with other students' as they learn about building better sentences for their writing. Ninth-grade English students volunteer information about the mnemonic devices and visualizations that they are using to remember the facts of *Romeo and Juliet* for the next day's exam. Ninth- and 10th-grade U.S. history students actively discuss today's news events and draw direct relations to the Supreme Court case, *Plessy vs. Ferguson.*

What do all of these snapshots have in common? They all show smart kids with learning difficulties actively involved in learning rigorous content and improving the skills that are affected by their learning disabilities, and they all took place one morning as we visited the Siena School, a private school in Silver Spring, MD.

The Siena School serves college-bound students who are challenged by language-based learning differences, such as dyslexia. Our observation of the school, and follow-up interview with the heads of the school, Jilly Darefsky and Clay Kaufman, provided further evidence of why Siena can serve as an example of how to put the four best practices for instruction of smart kids with learning difficulties into action.

Instruction in the student's area of strength. All of the high school courses at Siena are considered honors level courses. Reading, writing, and analytic skills are taught at a very high level. There is a senior independent project that is completed by every student. The first half of the year is spent preparing a research paper and the second half of the year is spent preparing a practical project related to the student's research. There is constant talk with students about their strengths throughout all grade levels. Students are helped to identify their strengths and then to utilize those strengths when they choose from alternatives of how to learn information and how to demonstrate that learning. Art is integrated in all academics, as a majority of the students demonstrate strengths in the arts. Cross-curricula connections help students to learn the answers to essential questions on a deeper level.

Instruction in skills and strategies in academic areas affected by the student's areas of challenge. Students are provided with instruction specific to improving areas affected by their disabilities, such as reading and writing. All teachers are trained in specific reading and writing strategies. Orton-Gillingham principles are used throughout the school. Teachers utilize a common vocabulary when teaching students. Reading methodology includes other evidence-based methods, such as the Lindamood-Bell Learning Processes. During the admissions process, there is extensive information shared about the student. Ongoing individualized planning for each student also occurs. Benchmark testing is done at least three times a year and more often for students who are not responding as quickly to the interventions. Reading teachers make adjustments every 1–2 weeks, grouping and regrouping students flexibly to meet their specific needs. As evidenced in our observations, the teaching of skills is also integrated into all content areas, so that students are improving those skills while learning challenging content.

Individualized instructional adaptations and accommodations systematically provided to students. Computers are in every classroom at Siena; at the high school level, all students have access to individual laptops. Students are taught keyboarding skills. A wide variety of assistive technology is available for students both during the school day and for homework. The assistive technology at Siena includes Kurzweil 3000 for reading and writing, Inspiration and Kidspiration for the organization of ideas for writing, and the use of Google Docs so that work can be done anywhere and quickly shared with instructors. Technology also provides support for the rigorous content that is taught throughout the program. Teachers frequently augment lessons with video clips from Discovery Education, an extensive bank of videos covering all content areas. Animation and film are utilized as part of the art integration throughout all courses. Teachers also utilize other adaptations in the classroom, such as mnemonics and visualization for memory. The use of a specially designed Siena planner, mind maps and other graphic organizers, study guides, and clearly, consistently posted goals, agenda, and homework, all support students with challenges in the areas of organization and study skills. As described in the snapshots above, active learning and use of inquiry is highly motivating for students and involves them more in their learning. Class size averages around 10 students with one instructor, allowing for significant teacher attention for each student.

Comprehensive case management to coordinate all aspects of the student's individual educational plan. Every Siena student has one teacher who serves as a case manager. Each case manager is responsible for advising six students. Student progress is reported to parents every 3 weeks. Teachers meet as a team on a regular basis, reviewing each student's progress together at least once a quarter. Students meet with their case manager every morning for 15 minutes to review the expectations of the school day. At the elementary and middle school level, students also meet with their case managers before they leave school for the day, chiefly for organizational support. In the high school, the last period of the day provides tutorial support for reading, writing, and math. Individual students can be assigned to this additional support or can seek it out on their own as needed. There are also eighth-period study halls and clubs available to students who are not involved in direct tutoring.

The Siena School is one example of many outstanding private and public programs throughout the United States that are meeting the needs of smart kids with learning difficulties. An analysis of these programs shows that they are successful when they fully implement the four areas of best practice, as illustrated above.

Trends in Public Schools

Over the past several years, there have been some decreases in public programming for smart kids with learning difficulties; however, at the same time, there have been increased efforts to train staff and the development of more private options. Several forces have coincided to lead to less special classroom programming in public schools. Perhaps the most obvious force is the national economic recession that has led to less funding being available for public schools. At the same time, two philosophical trends have also pushed in the same direction. The No Child Left Behind Act (2001) required that every child be taught by a teacher who is highly qualified in his or her subject area. To meet this requirement, many public schools have put an emphasis on including more students with disabilities in typical classrooms and bringing those supports into the classroom. This is done by having a special educator team teach (or coteach) with a highly qualified general education teacher or by bringing a paraprofessional into the general education classroom to support individual students. Other times, school districts have attempted to meet the needs of disabled students without additional staffing by providing accommodations to the individual students with disabilities and/or training to the general education staff.

One exception to the decrease of special classroom programs in the public schools has been in the area of classes and programs for students with autism. Many public schools have developed exemplary programs for student who are very bright and have high-functioning autism. MCPS's program for students with Asperger's syndrome is one example (a full description of that program can be found in Silverman and Weinfeld, 2007)

Although we are concerned about any steps backward to offering programs and services to smart kids with learning difficulties, we do applaud the move by several states to provide manuals and training for staff regarding the education of twice-exceptional students. In particular, over the past several years, Colorado, Idaho, and Virginia have produced statewide manuals. Maryland has been very active in providing online training to staff across the state. New York is presently considering legislation that would make training to staff a requirement.

Despite the decrease in public school special classroom options or perhaps because of it, the past few years has seen the development of many new private options. The *2e (Twice-Exceptional) Newsletter* is an outstanding resource, as well as the closest thing we have to a national clearinghouse for information about twice-exceptional students and programs. See the

Tools section of this chapter for a list of programs supporting twice-exceptional students compiled by this newsletter. Many of the schools that are listed come from parent or a single professional recommendation, so parents will want to research the individual school on their own.

Many private or independent schools do an excellent job of providing an appropriate education for bright students with learning challenges. Some of these schools have certified special education staff and are accredited by their states to implement students' IEPs. Other schools may not be state approved as special education schools, but still may do an outstanding job of providing the challenge, supports, and specialized instruction GT/LD students need.

When evaluating whether any private school may be a good fit for your child, parents should scrutinize the program in the same way you would a public school program. First, you will want to see the ways the school provides challenging instruction that will help your child to fulfill his or her potential. Secondly, you will need to look for evidence that teachers routinely employ a variety of adaptations and accommodations so that all students can access rigorous instruction. You will want to examine the strategies and interventions the schools use to help students improve their weaker academic areas, as well as their behavioral and attention skills, including self-advocacy skills. Finally, you will want to look for evidence of effective case management that brings you and the school staff together into a partnership for the benefit of the individual students.

The Internet has opened up a world of information to explore. Entering key words in a search engine will take you to an ever-expanding look at the programs and services that exist all over the United States for twice-exceptional students. For example, Northwestern University in Chicago offers a talent development program that serves twice-exceptional students; Idaho provides a resource book that is a framework for the identification of twice-exceptional students and includes implementation strategies for this targeted population; Minnesota offers a list of resources that support learners who are gifted and have additional exceptionalities; and the Bridges Academy in California is a college preparatory school for GT/

LD students in grades 5–12. Some interesting and helpful sites include:

- Davidson Institute for Talent Development Database—http://www.davidsongifted.org/DB
- "You Are Here": Talent Search Helps (Twice) Exceptional Student Succeed—http://www.ctd.northwestern.edu/resources/displayArticle/?id=338
- *Twice-Exceptional: Students With Both Gifts and Challenges or Disabilities*—http://www.sde.idaho.gov/site/gifted_talented/twice-exceptional/docs/2E%20Manual.pdf
- Minnesota Council for the Gifted and Talented/Resources—http://mcgt.net/twice-exceptional-2e
- Johns Hopkins University Center for Talented Youth (CTY)—http://www.cty.jhu.edu
- Jack Kent Cooke Foundation (provides funding for programs for gifted students who have challenges)—http://www.jkcf.org
- Learning Ally (formerly Recording for the Blind and Dyslexic)—http://www.LearningAlly.org

Additional helpful sites can be found in the Resources section of this book.

KEY POINTS

- The past few years have seen a decrease in special programming in public schools, an increase in public school staff training, and an increase in private options.
- Student programming should include challenging instruction, flexible grouping, and schedules that enable students to spend time with their intellectual peers for in-depth study in all subject areas.
- In the elementary years, opportunities for cluster groupings of bright students need to be created within individual classrooms or grade levels, and if needed, across grade levels.

- In the middle school years, gifted or advanced classes are good options for GT students with disabilities, as well as cluster grouping in all subject areas.
- In high school, there should be opportunities for GT/LD students to take honors and Advanced Placement courses in all of the major disciplines and in many of the electives offered.
- Bright students, especially those with learning challenges, must be provided opportunities that focus on their gifts, enabling them not only to develop a positive self-concept, but also the realization of their potential.
  - Look for schools and programs in which the four best practices are evident:
  - Instruction in the student's areas of strength
  - Instruction in skills and strategies that are affected by the student's disability
  - Appropriate adaptations and accommodations
  - Comprehensive case management that brings school and home together as a team and promotes self-advocacy on the part of the student

- Observe, reflect, and respond to student behaviors.
- Keep up with current programs and services.
- *2e Newsletter* serves as an excellent clearinghouse for updated information about programs for twice-exceptional students.

TIPS AND TOOLS

Supplementary materials included in this section:

- ➤ The Animal School: Bright Animals With Learning Difficulties

- ➤ Task Analysis Checklist for Programs and Services

- ➤ What to Look for in a School Checklist

- ➤ Program and Service Options Checklist

- ➤ Student and Parent Interviews

- ➤ 2E Resources

The Animal School: Bright Animals With Learning Difficulties

George Reavis wrote *The Animal School: A Fable* when he was the Assistant Superintendent of the Cincinnati Public Schools in the 1940s. Rich Weinfeld has adapted Reavis's fable to apply to smart kids with learning challenges. They each have a great educational message.

TIPS

Teacher

Read the fable to the class. Discuss the meaning. Give to parents at conference time. Use in training sessions.

Parent

Read the fable. Share with teachers and discuss the meaning. Share with your child. Discuss the meaning with your child and how it applies to issues he or she may be facing.

Student

Read the fable. Think about how it relates to you, a friend, or a person in your classroom or in your community activities.

The Animal School: Bright Animals With Learning Difficulties

Once upon a time, the animals decided they must do something to prepare their young to face the challenges of the world, and so they organized a school. They adopted an activity curriculum consisting of running, climbing, swimming, and flying, and to make sure all animals were competent in all of the important skills, all of the animals had to take all of the subjects.

The Duck was an excellent swimmer, better in fact than his instructor, and made passing grades in flying, but he was very poor in running. Because he was slow in running, he had to stay after school and also spend less time swimming, in order to spend more time practicing his running. This was continued until his webbed feet were badly worn and he was only average in swimming. But, average was acceptable in the new animal school, so nobody worried about that except the Duck.

The Rabbit started at the top of his class in running, but he had a nervous breakdown because of so much makeup work in swimming.

The Squirrel was excellent in climbing, until he developed frustration in the flying class, where his teacher made him start from the ground up instead of from the treetop down. His feelings of frustration spilled over to his other classes and he ended up with a C in climbing and a D in running.

The newest student in the school was an abnormal animal called the Snakehead Fish. At the end of the year the Snakehead, which could swim very well and also climb out of the water and walk on the land, was the valedictorian of the school.

Task Analysis Checklist for Programs and Services

The following task analysis illustrates the process that specialists undertake as they create rigorous and supportive programs for their bright underachieving students.

TIPS

Teacher

Use as a self-evaluation checklist. Use when you're planning accommodations for students. Use as a communication tool with parents, other staff members, and students.

Parent

Use as an evaluation tool of your child's school experience. Use it for creating questions to ask at conferences and other meetings.

Student

Look at the Task Analysis checklist to see if you want to add any information that would be important for your parents and teachers to know.

Task Analysis Checklist for Programs and Services

_____ Analyze what the roles and responsibilities of the educators are within the school.

_____ Assign the roles and responsibilities to the educators within the school.

_____ Set up a collaborative climate. Team planning facilitates inclusion of these students in the regular classroom.

_____ Collect and study data related to the students (e.g., test scores, performance in school, and performance in the community).

_____ Extend each child's intellectual boundaries and help all students achieve their highest potential.

_____ Identify and provide for students who have the capability, motivation, or potential to accept the challenges of honors, AP, and advanced-level courses the opportunity to do so.

_____ Focus on students' strengths and interests. Ensure that differentiated educational programs and/or services are systematically provided for bright students in all grades, including students with learning disabilities or other special needs.

_____ Provide accelerated and enriched instruction, including appropriate strategy and skill instruction, instructional adaptations, and accommodations, while implementing students' IEPs and/or 504 Plans.

_____ Analyze curricula to identify key concepts.

_____ Collect resources and materials (e.g., curricula guides, programs, software).

_____ Choose appropriate resources, materials, strategies, and techniques.

_____ Plan for alternative learning activities.

_____ Plan units and lessons.

_____ Collect appropriate adaptations and accommodations for each student.

_____ Implement units and lessons.

_____ Plan for assessments that capitalize on students' strengths and obviate weaknesses.

_____ Evaluate successful/best practices.

_____ Schedule team meetings to discuss students. Specific weekly, bimonthly, or monthly meeting times allow for ongoing planning and an opportunity to discuss and evaluate student progress. This way, difficulties are addressed before they multiply and escalate.

Task Analysis Checklist for Programs and Services, continued

_____ Know and understand the social/emotional profile of each student in order to provide strategies that alleviate frustration and create motivation and interest in school learning.

_____ Train teachers on aspects of smart students with learning challenges, including their characteristics, needs, strategies, adaptations, and accommodations.

_____ Train students and parents on available resources, materials, and strategies.

_____ Keep lines of communication open between and among staff, students, and parents.

What to Look For in a School Checklist

A school is a vibrant community of learners. The following checklist includes specifics that help define a good school environment.

TIPS

Teacher

Use the checklist as a positive evaluation tool for your school and classroom.

Parent

Use the checklist as a positive evaluation tool for your child's school. Talk to educators and other parents at your school about what makes a good school. Become involved as a volunteer. Keep a positive perspective.

What to Look for in a School Checklist

School Data

- Vision or mission statement _____
- Staff and staff supports _____
- Curriculum _____
- Level of academic rigor _____
- Extracurricular offerings _____
- Grading and reporting policy _____
- Test scores _____

Climate

- Positive tone _____
- Respect _____
- Comfort _____
- Supportive environment _____
- Students engaged in purposeful activities _____
- Challenging environment _____
- Interactive environment _____
- Risk-taking environment _____
- Flexible environment _____
- Visible standards and expectations _____
- Technologically up-to-date _____
- Open communication among educators, parents, and students _____

Organization

- Grouping _____
- Team teaching _____
- Flexible schedules _____

Programs

- Challenging instruction _____
- Flexible grouping and schedules _____
- Strength-based instruction _____
- Differentiated instruction _____

Management
- Consistent behavior expectations   _____
- High academic expectations   _____
- Collaborative   _____
- Positive reinforcement   _____
- Sense of humor   _____
- Timely feedback   _____
- Efficient record keeping   _____
- Evaluation   _____

Self-Advocacy Opportunities   _____

Attention to Social/Emotional Principles   _____

Variety of Materials, Resources, and Activities   _____

Program and Service Options Checklist

The following checklist should aid you in evaluating the GT/LD program in your school and other outside programs.

TIPS

Teacher

Use information to provide contacts and resources.

Parent

Use to guide decision making about programs for your child. Use to provide your school system with information about exemplary programs.

Student

Use to find out how kids like you are being challenged and supported in other places.

Program and Service Options Checklist

The following services and/or programs are examples of those that may be available in schools.

Local Public Schools

(Sources: school website, principal, counselor, GT specialist)

The school in consideration offers:

_____ Talent development programs

_____ GT/LD services

_____ GT services

_____ Special education services

Evidence of:

_____ instruction in the student's area of strength

_____ opportunities for the instruction of skills and strategies in academic areas that are affected by the student's challenges

_____ an appropriately differentiated program, including individualized instructional adaptations and accommodations systematically provided to students

_____ comprehensive case management to coordinate all aspects of the student's IEP

_____ rigorous instruction

_____ clear roles and responsibilities

_____ attention to social/emotional issues

Other Schools

(Sources: state department of education website, state GT coordinator, special education coordinator, private advocates)

Does the school in consideration offer:

_____ Talent development programs

_____ GT/LD services

_____ GT services

_____ Special education services

Program and Service Options
Checklist, continued

Evidence of:

_____ instruction in the student's area of strength

_____ opportunities for the instruction of skills and strategies in academic areas that are affected by the student's challenges

_____ an appropriately differentiated program, including individualized instructional adaptations and accommodations systematically provided to students

Student and Parent Interviews

When the focus of learning is on a student's strengths and interests, rather than on his or her areas of weakness, then self-confidence and self-esteem are increased and he or she is more likely to be successful. Interviews are one way to obtain information on students' strengths and interests.

TIPS

Teacher

Use the Student Interview questions to help you identify your student's strengths and interests. Use the Parent Interview questions to gain information about the student. When planning instruction for the student, work through these strengths whenever possible. The questions are also helpful when trying to match your student with a mentor.

Parent

Ask yourself the parent questions when trying to identify your child's strengths and interests. Share the information with the teacher.

Student

Ask yourself the student questions to help you identify your strengths and interests.

Parent Interview

1. What does your child choose to do in his or her free time?

2. What are your child's interests in school?

3. What are your child's interests outside of school?

4. What are your child's hobbies?

5. On what types of school projects are your child most successful?

6. What do you see as your child's strengths, abilities, or expertise?

7. What does your child like to talk about?

8. What does your child read about?

9. How does your child choose to show what he or she knows?

Student Interview

1. What do you choose to do in your free time?

2. What are your interests in school?

3. What are your interests outside of school?

4. What are your hobbies?

5. On what types of school projects are you most successful?

6. What do you see as your strengths, abilities, or areas of expertise?

7. What do you like to talk about?

8. What do you read about?

9. How do you choose to show what you know?

Student Interview, continued

10. If you could study anything that you wanted, what would you choose to study?

11. How did you become interested in this topic?

12. What have you done on your own (outside of school) in this area?

13. Would you like to work with a mentor (someone who helps you work on projects that interest you)? What is it about working with a mentor that appeals to you?

14. If you could study the topic from Question 10 with a mentor, what types of things are you interested in having a mentor do with you on this topic?

15. How do you like to learn? (For example, do you learn best through books, movies, museums, hands-on experiences, interviewing people, or other methods?)

16. What type of product do you like to develop best? (For example, do you prefer to do an essay, a poster, a movie, a PowerPoint™ presentation, a model, a speech, or another type of product?)

2e Resources: Schools and Programs for 2e Students

The *2e: Twice-Exceptional Newsletter* is an outstanding resource as well as the closest thing we have to a national clearinghouse for information about twice-exceptional students and programs. The following is a list that it currently has posted on its website (http://www.2enewsletter.com/topic_resources_schools-programs.html).

TIPS

Teacher

Read over this information to broaden your own knowledge base about programs in the United States.

Parent

Read over the listing of schools and programs as a starting point for your research into offerings across the country for twice-exceptional children.

2e Resources: Schools and Programs for 2e Students

The following information has been compiled by 2e: Twice-Exceptional Newsletter (http://www.2enewsletter.com) *based on information provided from its readers. We do not endorse any of these programs or schools, but merely offer them as a starting point for parents in their search for an appropriate learning environment for their children.*

Public Schools and School Districts with Programs that Directly Address the Needs of 2e Students

- Albuquerque School District, NM—an elementary-level program started by Drs. Dennis Higgins and Elizabeth Nielsen.
- Montgomery County, MD—Elementary and high school programs.
- A program offered by the Board of Cooperative Educational Services in Westchester County, NY.
- Cherry Creek School District, CO
- Howard County School District, MD
- Scottsdale, Arizona, Unified School District and offers a class for gifted with learning disabilities at Zuni Elementary
- Paradise Valley, Arizona, Unified School District #69 in Phoenix

Private Schools Specifically for 2e Kids

- Bridges Academy, a private college preparatory school for 2e kids in the Los Angeles area. Visit http://www.bridges.edu.
- The Lang School, an elementary/middle school in New York City. Visit http://www.thelangschool.org.

Private Schools Recommended to *2e Newsletter*

Name	Contact Information	Type of School	Comments
ASSETS School Honolulu, HI	http://www.assets-school.net	Day school for gifted and/or dyslexic students. Ages 5–18.	Recipient of a Jack Kent Cooke Foundation grant for its commitment to serving 2e students.
Benchmark School Philadelphia, PA	http://www.benchmark school.org	Day school. Ages 6–14.	Recommended by a parent.
Cambridge School of Weston Weston, MA	http://www.csw.org	Day and boarding school. Grades 9–12.	Recommended by a psychologist as a school that can address needs of 2e kids.
Centreville School Centreville, DE	http://www.centreville school.org	Day school. Ages 4–13.	Recommended by a parent. Provides individual educational program for learning-disabled children including integrated services of occupational and speech/language therapy for children. Also provides educational tutoring and therapy.
Chartwell School Seaside, CA	http://www.chartwell.org	Day school for students who have language-related visual and auditory learning challenges with the goal of helping them return successfully to mainstream education. Grades 2–8.	Recipient of a Jack Kent Cooke Foundation grant for its commitment to serving 2e students.
Chrysalis School Woodinville, WA	http://www.chrysalis-school. com/Home.htm	Day school. Grades K–12.	Recommended by a parent. See profile in 7/07 issue of 2e Newsletter.
Churchill Center and School for Learning Disabilities St. Louis, MO	http://www.churchillstl.org	Therapeutic day school for learning disabled children in elementary and middle school.	Recommended by a parent.

Private Schools Recommended to *2e Newsletter*, continued

Name	Contact Information	Type of School	Comments
Hampshire School Rindge, NH	http://www.hampshire countryschool.org	Boarding school. Boys only, ages 8–13.	Parent comments: "Can provide appropriate structure and support for certain students with nonverbal learning disabilities, Tourette Syndrome, ADHD, Asperger Syndrome, and other disorders; but it is not a treatment program."
Jemicy School Baltimore, MD	http://www.jemicyschool .org	Day school for college-bound students ages 6–18. Uses a multisensory curriculum to address dyslexia and other language-based learning differences.	Recipient of a Jack Kent Cooke Foundation grant for its commitment to serving 2e students.
John Dewey Academy Great Barrington, MA	http://www.jda.org	Boarding school. Grades 9–12.	Recommended by a psychologist as a therapeutic boarding school for gifted kids with emotional difficulties.
The Khabele School Austin, TX	http://www.thekhabele school.org	Day school. Grades 6–12.	Recommended by a parent.
The Lab School Washington, DC, and Baltimore, MD	http://www.labschool.org	Day school. Grades K–12. For children with average to gifted intelligence who also have dyslexia, language-based disabilities, and/or AD/HD. Teaches all areas of the curriculum through the arts.	Profiled in 11/08 issue of *2e Newsletter.*

Private Schools Recommended to *2e Newsletter*, continued

Name	Contact Information	Type of School	Comments
Lawrence School Broadview Heights, OH	http://www.lawrence school.org	Day school. Grades 1–12. For bright students with learning and attention differences.	Recipient of a Jack Kent Cooke Foundation grant for its commitment to serving 2e students.
The Marvelwood School Kent, CT	http://www.themarvelwood school.org	Boarding school. Grades 9–12.	Recommended by a psychologist as a school that can address needs of 2e kids.
Peabody School Albemarle County, VA	http://www.peabodyschool.org	Day school. Grades K–8.	Recommended by a parent.
Pilot School Wilmington, DE	http://www.pilotschool.org	Day school. Ages 5–14.	Recommended by a parent.
Winston School Dallas, TX	http://www.winston-school.org	Day school. Grades 1–12.	Recommended by a parent.

Public Charter School Recommended to *2e Newsletter*

Name	Contact Information	Type of School	Comments
City Academy Salt Lake City, Utah	http://www.cityacademyslc.org	Grades 7–12	Comment by parent: "I am very thrilled with how they are working with [my son's] strengths and challenges. I would recommend this as a school for parents of 2e kids in the Salt Lake area to consider."

In addition to the list above, Commonwealth Academy in Alexandria, VA, does a wonderful job of meeting the needs of college bound students with disabilities. The Auburn Schools of Herndon, VA, Silver Spring, MD and Baltimore, MD, do a great job of meeting the needs of bright students with social communication difficulties, including those with autism. The Model Asperger's Program at Ivymount School in Potomac, MD, is a state of the art program for smart students with mild autism. The staff and parents of one school that closed (The Norbel School) have opened up a new school, The Compass Academy in Halethorpe, MD. We encourage parents and professionals to provide information about other schools to the *2e Newsletter* so that it can continue to update its list.

Note. Adapted from "2e Resources: Schools and Programs for 2e Students," by *2E Newsletter*, 2013, http://www.2enewsletter.com/topic_resources_schools-programs.html. Copyright 2013 by *2E Newsletter*. Adapted with permission.

5

WHAT ACTIONS ENSURE THAT OUR SMART KIDS WILL OVERCOME THEIR LEARNING DISABILITIES?

Mr. and Mrs. Anderson were relieved and somewhat surprised as they left the team meeting for their son, Matthew, at his new school. Matthew was a complicated student with great gifts and significant challenges. In the past, they had received many contacts from the school about the problems that existed, but few positive comments or solutions. This year they had been called to come to the school before the year even began to plan for Matthew's first year in middle school.

Matthew's English teacher, who was also the sixth-grade team leader, volunteered to tell all of the staff about the appropriate adaptations and accommodations Matthew would need. The teacher described the special education instruction that she would be providing to address Matthew's needs in writing and organization. The team leader

   DOI:10.4324/9781003237983-6

would coordinate the communication between the general educators, Matthew, and his parents, as well as communicate regularly with the special education teacher. The team leader spoke about how bright Matthew was and that he should be involved in some GT classes.

The special educator said she would communicate with the counselor, who suggested that Matthew participate in a new group to help students advocate for themselves when talking with teachers about their strengths and needs. Matthew agreed to participate in the counseling group and to check in with the resource teacher at the beginning and end of each day to clarify his assignments and make sure he had the needed materials. Mr. and Mrs. Anderson agreed to check Matthew's planbook each night and communicate to staff via e-mail on a regular basis.

The team recommended that Matthew start the year in GT classes for science and social studies with a review before the second marking period began to evaluate his progress and to make recommendations for the next marking period. The principal reviewed each person's responsibilities and set the date for a progress review. Mr. and Mrs. Anderson and Matthew left the meeting feeling optimistic that the new school year would be Matthew's best yet.

Matthew's success that school year was aided by a team approach implemented by the educators who serve gifted students with learning disabilities in his home school. Whether a parent, teacher, or administrator, each person plays an important role in ensuring that our bright students with learning difficulties will overcome their obstacles and realize their potential. Each of us has a role in making it happen.

MAKING IT HAPPEN

Making It Happen in the Classroom

Designing a dynamic classroom where students are successful does not happen serendipitously. It requires careful analysis, planning, and thoughtful implementation. Key to its success is the educator's adoption of the underlying belief that these students are gifted first and their learning challenges come second. Once this is firmly embedded in one's attitude, developing a climate in which students feel safe and can achieve success is a natural outcome. Providing appropriate accommodations with the understanding that one is leveling the playing field rather than giving unfair advantage is also key to a students' success (Weinfeld et al., 2002).

General education teachers are expected to teach students who exhibit a wide range of needs. They often fail to identify twice-exceptional students, however, because these students may be able to compensate for their disabilities with their gift-edness. It is essential that the general education teacher know that gifts and disabilities often mask each other, and that these students are likely to exhibit variable performance and social/emotional difficulties (Landrum, 1989). These students may appear to possess average abilities, but are really performing well below their potential (Baum, 1990; Brody & Mills, 1997).

It is important for educators to keep in mind that the writing, organization, memory, and reading skills of these students are likely to impact their success across all subject areas. In planning, it is crucial that the teacher consider instructional methods and strategies that either circumvent the student's difficulties or that build in the necessary scaffolding to empower students to be successful with the demands of the assignment.

Educators can build in the necessary scaffolding by analyzing the obstacles that would prevent a student from accessing rigorous instruction. Once the student's obstacles have been identified, educators should reference the menu of possible interventions and choose those that will provide access to appropriate enriched and accelerated instruction (for more information, see the Bordering on Excellence materials at the end of Chapter 3).

Train teachers. The success of any program is dependent upon the training of those who work with twice-exceptional students. Training should focus on the definition, identification, and best practices to use in programming for these students. Some universities offer undergraduate and graduate courses specific to identification and appropriate services for bright students with learning disabilities. County, state, and national conferences or institutes on topics related to the instruction of these students also provide good training grounds for staff. Professional leave is often granted so educators may participate in these sessions, with the intent of learning the material and implementing it with their students. Training is also accomplished during school-based in-service workshops, staff meetings, and team or individual meetings.

During school-based, half-day or full-day training sessions, schools can address a variety of topics related to these students. The administrator, special education staff, counselor, GT staff, and grade-level teams should collaborate on meeting the needs of these students within the school. Based on a student's needs assessment, in-service workshops are designed to introduce and/or develop instructional resources, materials, and strategies to be used with students. For example, in-service workshops may include topics such as building positive attitudes; a deeper understanding of the characteristics, strengths, and needs of this population; conflict resolution strategies; strategies for integrating arts instruction into content areas; thinking strategies such as Bloom's (1956) taxonomy and Edward de Bono's (1986) Thinking Hats; utilizing mentors; and strategies on how to differentiate instruction. Training also should include a review of current successful practices in the areas of reading, writing, organization, memory, metacognition, and the use of technology.

Staff meetings are a good time for training. Due to the shorter length of this type of meeting, one concept, strategy, idea, or issue can be addressed. For example, keeping up-to-date on current research is important, so in this type of forum, a recent journal article related to GT/LD students may be distributed and discussed with staff members.

Team or individual meetings offer excellent opportunities for training. The resource teacher shares with a teacher or team an effective adaptation or accommodation for these students. In this setting, questions, concerns, and plans are focused on individual students and their specific strengths and needs. The immediate transfer and application of this type of training takes place in the classroom.

Within the school setting, each member has expertise in different areas. Share your knowledge with others. Advocate on behalf of twice-exceptional students for access to gifted programming and for the accommodations and special services that they need to be able to access higher level, more challenging classes. Become knowledgeable of tools and special programs that exist within your school system and in your community. Explore resources that will provide opportunities for students to develop their strengths, interests, and passions through mentoring, clubs, and activities in and out of school and share these with other staff members and parents.

Create a student snapshot. You probably have seen situations where a student struggles with one teacher and is successful with another. One teacher sees the strengths while the other does not. It is helpful to not only share what works, but also to capture the student's successes and knowledge you learn by working with him, so that when he moves from one teacher to the next or year to year, he does not have to start anew. As you discover "what works," the student's team can compile the information about the student's strengths and weaknesses, learning preferences, and successful accommodations into some type of document or "snapshot" that can be passed from teacher to teacher and year to year. Students could also carry a copy to use as a way to advocate for themselves. As parents, it is important to share your observations and information with the team (Shevitz et al., 2011).

Teach self-advocacy. Self-advocacy doesn't necessarily come naturally or easily, especially for twice-exceptional learners. It is a skill that has to be taught. Often frustrated and angry, these students do not understand their gifts and their needs. In our experience, two of the best predictors of success in high school and beyond for these students are positive self-concept and strong self-advocacy. A student who sees himself as a capable learner and is comfortable requesting and using accommodations that allow him to access class material can be successful, despite the learning obstacles that he faces. It is our responsibility to help these students acquire the skills to feel comfortable being their own advocate and provide opportunities for them to practice.

Tool 79: Student Profile: At-A-Glance

Name: _____

Strengths	Interests

Needs, Obstacles, Stumbling Blocks

Learning Style

Important Data and Instruments Used

Adaptations/Accommodations	Interventions

Instructional Strategies	

What Works	Other

Figure 9. Continued.

There are four stages to developing self-advocacy: developing self-awareness or understanding one's strengths and limitations; encouraging self-acceptance; promoting self-determination; and cultivating self-advocacy (Shevitz et al., 2011). The first step is helping students develop self-awareness, to understand their unique gifts and disabilities. Self-acceptance comes when students have a more clear understanding of who they are. As they find that there are other people, even famous people, who are like them, they begin to not only accept who they are, but realize there is a niche in the world for them. Self-determination comes into play when we allow and encourage students to start making decisions for themselves. As soon as they are ready, they should be included in IEP or 504 Plan meetings so that they can help determine what supports would work best for them. Eventually, students should be able to advocate on their own behalf, giving them the sense that they are in control of their future—which ultimately is our goal!

Use tools. In the introduction, we mentioned *101 School Success Tools for Smart Kids With Learning Difficulties,* a book to help teachers in their classrooms. This handbook gives teachers practical, hands-on tools and strategies to help recognize and nurture the potential in twice-exceptional students. The teacher is in the position to be able to serve as a catalyst, empowering these students to become successful learners. With the necessary resources and thorough understanding of these students, teachers can determine a precise educational direction and create a dynamic program that helps smart kids with learning difficulties overcome their obstacles and realize their potential. Using tools like the ones in the above-mentioned book can help.

Making It Happen at Home

The parent-school partnership is critical in helping ensure that your child gains an awareness of his strengths and an understanding and acceptance of his areas of need. As parents, you are often the first to recognize your child's gifts and learning difficulties. Your role in communicating to teachers what you know about your child is critical in facilitating their role in ensuring that students receive the support they need. As we have mentioned earlier, you are your child's first teacher. You have knowledge of your child's emotional, intellectual, and creative mind that may or may not be evident in the school setting. You are the link between your child and the school community and, just as it is the teacher's role to keep you informed of your child's progress and growth in class, it is your responsibility to provide the missing pieces and insight into how you see his strengths and share his interests. By providing this additional information, the teacher has a window into what makes him tick, what works, what shuts him down, and what he needs to be successful. Be sure that your information is included in the "snapshot" that gets passed to the next teacher. Also, share things that your child is involved in outside of school. From your information, teachers will now able to glean a better profile of your child and draw on his interests when presenting materials, offering alternative projects, and making connections to his world.

Explore options and opportunities in your school and community. Take advantage of the resources around you that play into your child's strengths and provide enriching experiences for her. Seek out opportunities that can build on her interests and passions and expose her to many types of experiences. Through these experiences, your child will be able to discover strengths that may not have the chance of revealing themselves within the classroom walls. Find a way to share strengths and passions with the school. Being successful in and out of school will help to build her self-esteem and self-determination.

Seek out a mentor for your child. A mentor can be a powerful influence in your child's life. If your school does not have a mentor program, meet with the principal and find out what it would take to start one. Draw on the resources within your school and community to obtain people interested in becoming a mentor. If your school does not have the resources, try to find a mentor for your child yourself. Talk to your child about the kinds of things she might like to learn; observe the kinds of television shows she watches, the questions she asks, and the types of books to which she is drawn. Search for someone who shares your child's passion. Investigate people or businesses in your area who may know someone willing to work with your child. MENTOR (http://www.mentor.org) is a national organization that can provide you with a wealth of information on how to start a program or help you find programs already exist in your area. A mentor can be the pivotal point in a child's belief in himself that he can be successful.

You need only to Google the phrase "enrichment programs for gifted students" to find an array of opportunities for your child. In addition, websites of national organizations like National Association for Gifted Children and those for the state departments of education are excellent places to help you begin your search for enrichment opportunities for your child.

From there, look for programs and experts in your local community.

Many colleges and universities offer Saturday and/or summer enrichment programs for gifted and talented youth. For example, Johns Hopkins University, the University of Virginia, Western Kentucky University, and the College of William and Mary all offer varied enrichment experiences designed to provide opportunities for students to explore topics of interest. Through online courses and satellite campuses, schools such as these are able to link students across the country to mentors and enrichment opportunities. In addition, college and university-based programs usually recognize the needs of twice-exceptional students, providing all students access to the programs.

Review publications that may appeal to your child. For example, Johns Hopkins University's Center for Talented Youth publishes the Parent's Choice Gold Award-winning magazine entitled *Imagine* for grades 7–12, which invites students to explore topics in science, arts, and humanities. Written by both gifted students and experts in different fields, each issue includes career profiles, students' creative work, and articles written by student about competitions and summer programs.

Also look to your local art museums, libraries, nature and community centers, and youth organizations as possible resources for enrichment activities and even a source for mentors. Finally, observe and take clues from your child about what she enjoys. The key to "making it happen" is helping your child discover her interests and passions and providing her with various opportunities to pursue them.

Develop and Initiate Action Plans to Make It Happen

The following plans of action are designed for educators, parents, and students. There are four consistent components: training, collaborative formulation of educational plans, ongoing communication, and evaluation. Each of these is crucial if effective adaptations and accommodations are to be provided to bright students with learning challenges.

Action Plan for Educators

1. Special educators and general educators should complete training on:
   a. the definition, identification, and best practices in programming for twice-exceptional students and bright underachieving students;
   b. understanding the assessment data that relates to these students;
   c. understanding appropriate resources, materials, strategies, and techniques to be used both in instruction and assessments that allow students to demonstrate their skills without the interference of their disabilities;
   d. understanding how to capitalize on students' strengths; and
   e. the need to evaluate and revise adaptations and accommodations.

2. Include general educators as part of the IEP, 504 plan, or child study team while formulating adaptations and accommodations.
3. Schedule ongoing face-to-face meetings between special educators and general educators to plan for implementation of the student's IEP, 504 plan, or child study plan, including needed adaptations and accommodations. Meetings should include a discussion of the reason for each adaptation and accommodation as it relates to the individual student's disability.
4. Build in an evaluation component to look at the efficacy of each adaptation and accommodation with a plan of fading them out over time, allowing students to move from dependence to independence.

Action Plan for Parents

1. Parents should participate in training on:
   a. the definition, identification, and best practices in programming for their children;

    b. the possible negative effects of providing excessive or unnecessary accommodations;

    c. the need to select accommodations based on the impact of the individual student's disability or learning challenges;

    d. the need to move students from dependence to independence; and

    e. the need to evaluate and revise adaptations and accommodations.

2. Parents should take part in the IEP, 504 plan, or child study team while it is formulating adaptations and accommodations.

3. Ongoing face-to-face meetings between school staff members and parents should occur to monitor implementation of the student's plan, including needed adaptations and accommodations.

4. Build in an evaluation component to look at the efficacy of each adaptation and accommodation with a plan of fading them out over time, allowing students to move from dependence to independence.

Action Plan for Students

1. Students should participate in training that stresses:

    a. understanding their own unique strengths and weaknesses;

    b. understanding how specific adaptations and accommodations maximize their strengths, while minimizing their weaknesses;

    c. understanding and implementing advocacy and communication strategies; and

    d. understanding the need to move from dependence to independence.

2. Include students as part of the IEP, 504 plan, or child study team, in the formulation of adaptations and accommodations.

3. Schedule ongoing face-to-face meetings between

school staff and students to monitor implementation of the student's plan, including needed adaptations and accommodations.

4. Ensure student participation in a periodic evaluation component to look at the efficacy of each adaptation and accommodation with a plan of fading them out over time, allowing students to move from dependence to independence.

FROM LD TO PH.D.:
POSTSECONDARY EDUCATION

What happens to smart kids with learning difficulties when they leave high school? Most of them go to colleges and universities and grow into productive, creative young professionals. Their choice in schools is as diverse as they are, from 2- and 4-year institutions, to art and trade institutes, to Ivy League universities. Their stories are inspiring and their accomplishments are extraordinary. They have stories of unleashed potential and realized dreams, where it is OK to imagine a world without barriers, and to set seemingly unattainable goals. These are talented young people who have overcome the barriers and frustrations that come with having learning difficulties or attention problems.

All students face the challenge of finding the right place to continue with their postsecondary education. Parents and kids need to know that there are wonderful schools to meet a variety of student needs, as well as the support to help find the right one for your child. Libraries and bookstores have reference guides to colleges and universities for students with learning and attention difficulties. There are professionals who specialize in working with students and families during the process of selecting and applying to schools.

The broad range of school choices that exists for all students also exists for students with learning difficulties, whether it is a large university in a city or rural setting or a small liberal arts college in the suburbs. There is also a wide range of student services available regardless of the size or location of the schools. It is important, however, to determine the type of school desired, and then find out which of these has the support that will best suit their needs.

All schools receiving federal funding must be in compliance with Section 504 of the Rehabilitation Act, which means they must provide accommodations for students with documented disabilities. Some schools will have whole departments and learning centers for their students. Others will have a mentor or case manager who helps students work with faculty to have their needs met. Some smaller schools will have a culture that is nurturing and supportive of all students that enables those with special needs to thrive. There are also schools that have programs, often at an additional cost, that give direct instruction to students to maximize their adjustment and success to college. These programs act as a bridge between high school and college for students with greater needs. For any of these supportive options to be successful, students must not only be open and available to the interventions, but they should have had the benefit and experience of having advocated for themselves in high school. Students who have become effective advocates accept their disability and recognize and know the accommodations that they need. These are the students who ultimately will be the most successful in school and life.

KEY POINTS

- A home/school partnership is essential.
- Self-advocacy is a key ingredient for student success.
- A dynamic classroom where students are successful requires careful analysis, planning, and thoughtful implementation.
- Critical to each teacher's success is the educator's adoption of the underlying belief that these students are gifted first and their learning challenges come second.
- Once this belief is firmly embedded in one's attitude, developing the climate in which the students feel safe and can achieve success is a natural outcome.

- Providing appropriate accommodations with the understanding that one is leveling the playing field rather than giving unfair advantage is also key to their success.
- The success of any program is dependent upon the training of those who work with GT/LD students. Training should focus on the definition, identification, and best practices to use in programming for these students.
- Teachers, parents, and students must develop clear and concise action plans and put them into practice.

TIPS AND TOOLS

Supplementary materials included in this section:

> ➤ College Planning

> ➤ Self-Advocacy

> ➤ Intervention Plan for Smart Kids With Learning Difficulties

College Planning

The checklist that follows should be used by gifted students with learning disabilities when planning for and evaluating college programs.

TIPS

Teacher

Talk with the school's media specialist or guidance department about purchasing some college reference guides for student and parent use. Organize a program to discuss college choices and available resources. Invite alumni to come and speak with your students and their parents about their experiences of selecting and attending colleges.

Parent

Be an active participant in the college selection process. Set clear parameters around which your child can make choices, including cost and distance.

Student

Meet with your guidance counselor in spring of your junior year to begin planning for postsecondary school. Be clear about what you need and want in a school, and begin planning early.

College Planning

Talk to high school counselors or private counselors who work with students with learning difficulties and students who have been through the college search.

Options I am considering:

   2-year colleges:

   4-year colleges:

   Technical:

Level of competitiveness:

Location:

Size:

College Planning, Continued

Special services I need in a college:

_____ Departments and learning centers dedicated to serving students with special needs

_____ Mentors/case managers

_____ Programs providing direct instruction

_____ Other services I need: _____

_____

_____

_____

Services available at the college I'm considering:

_____ Departments and learning centers dedicated to serving students with special needs

_____ Mentors/case managers

_____ Programs providing direct instruction

_____ Other services I need: _____

_____

_____

_____

Notes:

Self-Advocacy

Self-advocacy is when students let others know about who they are and what they need. Learning and practicing strategies for developing self-advocacy make it possible for these students to become risk takers and lifelong learners. Over time, students develop the skills and maturity that allow them to become partners in decision making regarding their IEPs.

TIPS

Teacher

Use this tool with students to help them identify their strengths and needs. Conference with students so you both gain an understanding of their strengths and needs. Provide an opportunity for students to practice their self-advocacy skills (i.e., role-playing, simulations).

Parent

Use this tool with your child to help identify her strengths and needs. Provide an opportunity for your child to practice self-advocacy skills.

Student

Fill out the tool sheet. Talk to your parents and teachers and practice self-advocacy skills at home and at school.

Self-Advocacy: What Defines Me as a Successful Learner?

Who I am (strengths and needs):

_____

_____

_____

_____

_____

_____

What I need (adaptations and accommodations):

_____

_____

_____

_____

_____

_____

Which tools work for me (interventions and strategies)?

_____

_____

_____

_____

_____

_____

How to get what I need to succeed:

_____

_____

_____

_____

_____

_____

Intervention Plan for Smart Kids With Learning Difficulties

The following tool is a sample intervention plan that can be used with gifted and learning disabled students. Check with your school district, as many have preset tools in place for developing intervention plans for students.

TIPS

Teacher

Use to analyze what is currently in place for the student and to make a plan of what could be done.

Parent

Use to analyze all aspects of what currently is in place for your child and to make a plan of what could be done.

Student

Use to understand your strengths and needs and give input to parents and teachers about your plan.

Intervention Plan for Smart Kids With Learning Difficulties

Name:

Date:

School:

A. Evidence of Gifts:

Test scores:

Performance in school:

(When does the student show interest, perseverance, self-regulation, and outstanding achievement?)

Performance in the community:

Evidence of Learning Difficulties:

(reading, writing, organization, memory, specific learning disabilities, ADHD)

Test scores:

Performance in school:

Behavioral/Attentional Problems:

Performance in school:

Performance at home:

Intervention Plan for Smart Kids With Learning Difficulties, Continued

B. **Current Program:**

Gifted instruction:

Adaptations:

Accommodations:

Special instruction:

Behavior/attention management:
(Plans, medication)

Counseling:
(In-school, therapy)

Case management:
(Home to school communication; communication among staff)

Intervention Plan for Smart Kids With Learning Difficulties, Continued

C. Recommendations:

Gifted instruction:

Adaptations:

Accommodations:

Special instruction:

Behavior/attention management:

Case management:

D. Next Steps:

CONCLUSION

"Not every child has an equal talent or an equal ability or an equal motivation, but children have the equal right to develop their talent, their ability, and their motivation."—John F. Kennedy

In the conclusion of the first edition of *Smart Kids With Learning Difficulties*, published in 2006, we stated:

It is important to think about what the future holds for bright students with learning challenges. A view of the future as seen by Ray Kurzweil (1999) and by Thomas West (1991) may shape how these students are educated today. Rapid development of technology is providing us with a new age of learning and retrieving information. Ray Kurzweil, a brilliant futurist, describes a society in his book, *The Age of Spiritual Machines,* where students interact extensively with computers. He predicts that, by the end of this decade, students will carry thin tablet like devices, for creating and accessing print materials either by voice or by pointing and clicking. Thomas West, in his book, *In the Mind's Eye,* says that it is these students who have made and will make some of the most extraordinary contributions to the world. He predicts that in the 21st century these students, many of whom possess outstanding abstract reasoning and visual-spatial abilities, will take the lead in many important endeavors. Their corresponding weaknesses in rote memory and organization will become insignificant, as technology fulfills those roles. (pp. 171–172)

Great strides have been made in the last 8–10 years. Ray Kurzweil's vision of students with their thin tablets is our new reality. With technological advances, our students do not have to feel awkward or stand out by using the computer as an accommodation, as it is now the way of the world. What was once an important accommodation that some students were reticent to use for fear of being different is now the norm and all are eager to have the latest, fastest, best technology to help with their work. Everyone is "working smarter," and this power in the hands of our twice-exceptional students will be instrumental to their success.

A majority of the students who have been identified and served during their elementary and secondary years will attend and graduate from college. Many of them will attend universities that are willing and able to provide appropriate accommodations, mentors, and other supports. The majority of these students will experience success that capitalizes on their strengths and minimizes their weaknesses in their chosen careers in fields such as the arts, engineering, the sciences, and architecture.

As parents, educators, and mentors, each of us has the responsibility and power to help these children realize their potential and to make their dreams come true. Samantha Abeel, in her book *Reach for the Moon*, eloquently writes of the impact that we can have on these students.

> When the plain brown seed was planted, you could already smell the fragrance of the flower that was to come, and you were proud as a good gardener should be. Thank you for believing that there was a flower waiting inside and for taking the time to help and watch it grow. When the sun rose from under its misty veil, you were there to watch, and I am thankful. (p. 39)

GLOSSARY

accommodations: procedure or enhancement that empowers a person with a disability to complete a task that he or she would otherwise be unable to complete because of a disability.

adaptations: modification to the delivery of instruction or materials used with a student.

alternative products: giving students choices; examples include oral presentations, models, and other visual representations.

anchor papers: good examples of student work that reflect expectations of the rubric.

arts integration: the inclusion of music, dance, the visual arts, and theatre into English, social studies, science, mathematics, or any subject to enhance the material.

assistive technology: tools that enhance and assist students' ability to achieve individual goals.

audio spell check: computer software that pronounces a word to help with spelling.

audiotape: a recording that enables students to hear print material; a way for students to demonstrate their understanding.

Bloom's taxonomy: the ordered steps of thinking created by Benjamin Bloom—knowledge, comprehension, application, analysis, synthesis, evaluation.

case management: the process of monitoring a student's instructional program including communication to and among students, parents, and appropriate school staff; monitoring of goals; and scheduling of timely meetings when needed.

charter school: a school funded with public money (except for the facilities) that is an alternative to regular public school systems.

Edward de Bono: one of the leading authors on the process of thinking, who believes thinking is a skill that can be learned, practiced, and improved.

decoding: breaking words down into discreet sounds to facilitate word recognition, pronunciation, and spelling.

differentiation: a kind of instruction that acknowledges commonalities and differences in the teaching and learning process; it is proactive, more qualitative than quantitative, and a blend of whole-class, group, and individual instruction that is student centered.

dramatization: a role-play, skit, reenactment, or simulation.

electronic organizers: a device that helps to organize and plan for upcoming assignments and events.

electronic spellers: a compact device that provides the correct spelling.

emotional overexcitability: refers to an emotional richness in creatively and intellectually gifted children that is characterized by strong emotions and reactions to their inner conflict between the world as it is and the world as they perceive it should be.

empower: behavior that promotes personal growth and increased competencies, increases a person's sense of control over life events, and/or encourages new coping abilities to replace maladaptive behavior (St. Edward's University, n.d.).

enable: behavior that interferes with acquisition of new competencies, reduces a person's sense of self-control over life events (self-efficacy), and/or reinforces old or maladaptive behavior (St. Edward's University, n.d.).

fixed mindset: a belief system that states that intelligence is a fixed trait, and because we can't really change how smart we are, some students will always be smart, and some will not.

gifted: possessing outstanding abilities in the areas of general intellectual capabilities, specific academic aptitudes, or the arts.

graphic organizer: a visual tool that a student uses to record information, ideas, or concepts to help organize information for prewriting or note taking.

grapho-motor: relating to or affecting movements made in writing.

growth mindset: a belief system that intelligence is a malleable quality, a potential that can be developed through effort and good instruction.

interdisciplinary approach: a method of teaching that incorporates two or more academic areas that are usually taught separately (i.e., combining history and art or English, science, and social studies).

KWL chart: a chart used to record what a student knows, wants to learn, and learns about a specific topic.

learning disability: Any of various cognitive, neurological, or psychological disorders that affects the ability to learn, especially one that interferes with the ability to learn mathematics or develop language skills.

metacognition: thinking about thinking, the awareness of one's thinking and cognitive processes.

mind-mapping: a visual tool used to organize one's thinking about a specific topic or concept.

modifications: adjustments made in assignments that address the student's needs/areas of weakness in order to help the student be successful (i.e., shorten assignments, allow a student to dictate rather than write).

mnemonic devices: a tool such as a formula or rhyme used to aid one's memory.

multiple modalities: a combination of senses, such as vision and hearing.

multisensory approach: a style of teaching that incorporates a combination of senses, such as vision, hearing, touch, and kinesthetic.

NCR paper: carbonless copying paper that allows a student to take notes on the top sheet and transfers it onto a second sheet; useful when a classmate is providing notes for a student with grapho-motor difficulties.

organizational software: computer software that assists students in writing by automatically organizing notes into outline form.

pencil grips: a rubber or sponge-like object that slides on a pencil and provides a better grip for students with grapho-motor difficulties.

perfectionism: a combination of thoughts and behaviors associated with high expectations for one's own performance.

portable keyboards: small, relatively inexpensive, lightweight, and durable keyboards that have the capability of storing information, but typically don't have the capacity to install software.

portfolio: an ongoing collection of products, representing a student's best work, and reflecting his or her strengths.

preassessment: a measurement taken before beginning a unit or course of study to determine a student's knowledge and the need for the instruction that is about to occur.

Response to Intervention (RtI): a collection of procedures used to determine how students respond to specific changes in general education instruction and provide a process for data-based decision making for creating, implementing, and evaluating appropriate interventions to improve student success.

rubric: clearly stated criteria that serves as a means for evaluating students and for guiding their work toward the desired product.

rule-based approach to reading: instruction that is based on students learning and practicing principles that can then be generalized to new material.

scaffolding: a framework to build in necessary subskills that will prepare students for the skill to be taught.

slant board: a tool that eases the physical effort required for handwriting, particularly used for students with grapho-motor issues.

speech-to-text software: computer software that allows the user's speech to be converted directly into print.

spell checker: a computer software program available as part of most writing programs that allows the user to check his or her spelling and replace misspelled words.

storyboards: used professionally by animators and movie makers; the process of students drawing the scenes of a story either as a first step toward writing or as an end product that demonstrates understanding.

story starters: prompts that provide the idea that a student will then elaborate upon in composing a written product.

study guide: a tool for helping students locate and focus on the information that the teacher has determined is crucial for preparing for an assessment.

task analysis: determination of all of the steps that are required to complete a given work assignment.

text-to-speech software: computer software that allows the user to transfer print material into speech and listen to it.

thematic units: an overarching theme or concept that connects the learning objectives amongst the disciplines.

think alouds: a teaching method that models the problem-solving or thought process that the individual may use to arrive at an answer or solution.

Universal Design for Learning: a practice that removes the obstacles to accessing instruction for all students and is built into all curriculum planning.

Venn diagram: a specific type of graphic organizer that compares several items and how they relate to one another.

visual imagery: creating pictures in one's mind that serve to clarify concepts and enhance the memory of the concepts.

voice recognition software: another name for speech-to-text software that allows users' speech to be converted directly into print.

webs: a specific type of graphic organizer.

word bank: to aid with memory or spelling issues; a list of words provided to the student from which he chooses in order to complete a writing assignment or assessment.

word prediction software: computer software that provides alternatives of the words that the user may be looking for after he or she types the initial letters of a word or the initial words in a sentence.

RESOURCES

PRINT RESOURCES

Alley, G., & Deschler, D. (1979). *Teaching the learning disabled adolescent: Strategies and methods*. Denver, CO: Love.

Baldwin, L. J., & Gargiulo, D. A. (1983). A model program for elementary age learning disabled/gifted youngsters. In L. H. Fox, L. Brody, & D. Tobin (Eds.), *Learning disabled/gifted children: Identification and programming* (pp. 207–221). Austin, TX: PRO-ED.

Baum, S. (1994). Meeting the needs of gifted/learning disabled students: How far have we come? *Journal of Secondary Gifted Education, 5*, 6–16.

Beckley, D. (1998). *Gifted and learning disabled: Twice exceptional students.* Storrs: University of Connecticut, The National Research Center on the Gifted and Talented.

Bees, C. (1998). The GOLD program: A program for gifted learning disabled adolescents. *Roeper Review, 21,* 155–161.

Betts, G. T. (1985). *Autonomous learner model.* Greeley, CO: ALPS.

Clements, C., Lundell, F., & Hishinuma, E. S. (1994). Serving the gifted dyslexic and gifted at risk. *Gifted Child Today, 17*(4), 12–14, 16–17, 36–37.

Coleman, M. R., & Gallagher, J. J. (1995). State identification policies: Gifted students from special populations. *Roeper Review, 17,* 268–275.

Daniels, P. R. (1983). *Teaching the gifted/learning disabled child.* Rockville, MD: Aspen Press.

Daniels, S., & Peters, D. B. (2013). *Raising creative kids.* Tuscon, AZ: Great Potential Press.

de Bono, E. (1986). *The CoRT thinking program.* Easterville, OH: SRA.

Dunst, C., & Trivette, C. (1987). Enabling and empowering families: Conceptual and intervention issues. *School Psychology Review, 16,* 443–456.

Eide, B. L., & Eide, F. F. (2012). *The dyslexic advantage: Unlocking the potential of the dyslexic brain.* New York, NY: Plume.

Ellston, T. (1993). Gifted and learning disabled . . . a paradox? *Gifted Child Today, 16,* 17–19.

Fall, J., & Nolan, L. (1993). A paradox of personalities. *Gifted Child Today, 16,* 46–49.

Fetzer, E. (2000). The gifted/learning-disabled child: A guide for teachers and parents. *Gifted Child Today, 23*(4), 44–50.

Fine, L. (2001a). Diamonds in the rough. *Education Week, XXI*(8), 38, 39, 41.

Fine, L. (2001b). Mining Maryland's diamonds: One district's solution. *Education Week, XXI*(8), 40.

Fisher, J. E., & Price, J. (2012). *Take control of dyslexia & other reading difficulties: The ultimate guide for kids.* Waco, TX: Prufrock Press.

Fox, L. H., Brody, L., & Tobin, D. (Eds.). (1983). *Learning disabled/gifted children: Identification and programming.* Austin, TX: PRO-ED.

Gentry, M., & Neu, T. W. (1998). Project High Hopes summer institute: Curriculum for developing talent in students with special needs. *Roeper Review, 20,* 291–295.

Grimm, J. (1998). The participation of gifted students with disabilities in gifted programs. *Roeper Review, 20,* 285–286.

Hammill, D. D. (1990). On defining learning disabilities: An emerging consensus. *Journal of Learning Disabilities, 23,* 74–84.

Hishinuma, E. S., & Nishimura, S. T. (2000). Parent attitudes on the importance and success of integrated self-contained services for students who are gifted, learning disabled, and gifted/learning disabled. *Roeper Review, 22,* 241–250.

Howard, J. B. (1994). Addressing needs through strengths: Five instructional practices for use with gifted/learning disabled students. *Journal of Secondary Gifted Education, 5,* 23–34.

Hughes-Lynch, C. E. (2010). *Children with high-functioning autism: A parents' guide.* Waco, TX: Prufrock Press.

Hughes-Lynch, C. E. (2011). *Teaching children with high-functioning autism: Strategies for the inclusive classroom.* Waco, TX: Prufrock Press.

LeVine, E., & Evans, M. J. (1983). The behaviorally disordered creative child: A challenge to our diagnostic and teaching procedures. *Contemporary Education, 55,* 28–32.

Maker, C. J. (1977). *Providing programs for the gifted handicapped.* Reston, VA: Council for Exceptional Children.

Maker, C. J. (1981). Problem solving strategies: A general approach to remediation. In D. D. Smith (Ed.), *Teaching the learning disabled* (pp. 132–166). Englewood Cliffs, NJ: Prentice-Hall.

Marland, S. P. (1972). *Education of the gifted and talented* (Report to the subcommittee on education, Committee on Labor and Public Welfare, U.S. Senate). Washington, DC: U.S. Government Printing Office.

Montgomery County Public Schools. (1998). *State of the art.* Rockville, MD: Author.

Montgomery County Public Schools. (1994). *Conflict resolution tools: Elementary version, teaching through the curriculum.* Rockville, MD: Author.

Montgomery County Public Schools. (2004). *Twice-exceptional students: A guidebook for supporting the achievement of gifted students with special needs.* Rockville, MD: Author.

Nielsen, M. E., Higgins, L. D., Wilkinson, S. C., & Webb, K. W. (1994). Helping twice-exceptional students to succeed in high school. *Journal of Secondary Gifted Education, 5,* 35–39.

Nielsen, M. E., & Mortorff-Albert, S. (1989). The effects of special education service on the self-concept and school attitude of learning disabled/gifted students. *Roeper Review, 12,* 29–35.

Norton, S., Hartwell-Hunnicut, K., & Norton, R. (1996). The learning disabled/gifted student. *Contemporary Education, 68,* 36–40.

Ogle, D. M. (1986). K-W-L: A teaching model that develops action reading of expository text. *The Reading Teacher, 40,* 564–570.

Price, J., & Fisher, J. E. (2010). *Take control of Asperger's syndrome: The official strategy guide for teens with Asperger's syndrome and nonverbal learning disorder.* Waco, TX: Prufrock Press.

Putnum/Northern Westchester Board of Cooperative Educational Services. (n.d.). *The gifted handicapped mentor program.* Yorktown Heights, NY: Author.

Reis, S. M., Neu, T. W. & McGuire, J. M. (1995). *Talents in two places: Case studies of high ability students with learning disabilities who have achieved* (Research Monograph 95114). Storrs: University of Connecticut, The National Research Center on the Gifted and Talented.

Rivera, D. B., Murdock, J., & Sexton, D. (1995). Serving the gifted/learning disabled. *Gifted Child Today, 18*(6), 34–37.

Rowe, A., Pace, J. F., & Tulchinsky-Cohen, K. (2013). *Creating effective programs for gifted students with learning disabilities.* Waco, TX: Prufrock Press.

Shevitz, B. R., Stemple, M., Barnes-Robinson, L., & Jeweler, S. (2011). *101 school success tools for smart kids with learning difficulties.* Waco, TX Prufrock Press.

Silverman, S., Iseman, J., & Jeweler, S. (2009). *School success for kids with ADHD.* Waco, TX: Prufrock Press.

Silverman, S., & Weinfeld, R. (2007). *School success for kids with Asperger's syndrome.* Waco, TX: Prufrock Press.

Simpson, C. G., & Spencer, V. G. (2009). *College success for students with learning disabilities.* Waco, TX: Prufrock Press.

Southern, W. T., & Jones, E. D. (1991). *The academic acceleration of gifted children.* New York, NY: Teachers College Press.

Spodak, R., & Stefano, K. (2011). *Take control of ADHD: The ultimate guide for teens with ADHD.* Waco, TX: Prufrock Press.

Suter, D. P., & Wolf, J. S. (1987). Issues in the identification and programming of the gifted/learning disabled child. *Journal for the Education of the Gifted, 10,* 227–237.

Thrailkrill, C. (1998). Patrick's story: A gifted/learning-disabled child. *Gifted Child Today, 21*(3), 24–27.

Torgesen, J. K. (1986). Computer assisted instruction with learning disabled students. In J. K. Torgesen & B. Y. L. Wong (Eds.), *Psychological and educational perspectives on learning disabilities* (pp. 417–435). Orlando, FL: Academic Press.

Trail, B. A. (2010). *Twice-exceptional children: Understanding, teaching, and counseling gifted students.* Waco, TX: Prufrock Press.

Udall, A. J., & Maker, C. J. (1983). A pilot program for elementary age learning disabled/gifted students. In L. H. Fox, L. Brody, & D. Tobin (Eds.), *Learning disabled/gifted children: Identification and programming* (pp. 223–242). Austin, TX: PRO-ED.

Vaughn, S. (1989). Gifted learning disabilities: Is it such a bright idea? *Learning Disabilities Focus, 4,* 123–126.

Waldron, K. A., Saphire, D. G., & Rosenblum, S. A. (1987). Learning disabilities and giftedness: Identification based on self-concept. *Journal of Learning Disabilities, 20,* 422–432.

Whitmore, J., & Maker, J. (1985). *Intellectual giftedness in disabled persons.* Rockville, MD: Aspen Press.

Will, M. (1986). *Educating students with learning problems: A shared responsibility.* Washington, DC: U.S. Department of Education.

Webb, J. T., & Latimer, D. (1993). *ADHD and children who are gifted.* ERIC EC Digest #E522. Reston, VA: ERIC Clearinghouse on Disabilities and Gifted Education.

Winebrenner, S. (1996). *Teaching kids with learning difficulties in the regular classroom.* Minneapolis, MN: Free Spirit.

Yewchuk, C., & Bibby, M. A. (1988). A comparison of parent and teacher nomination of gifted hearing-impaired students. *American Annals of the Deaf, 133,* 344–348.

WEBSITES

2e (Twice-Exceptional) Newsletter—http://www.2enewsletter.com

All Kinds of Minds—http://www.allkindsofminds.org

Association for the Education of Gifted Underachieving Students—http://www.aegus.org

Autism Society of America—http://www.autism-society.org

Center For Talented Youth, Johns Hopkins University—http://www.jhu.edu/~gifted

Children and Adults With Attention Deficit/Hyperactivity Disorder—http://www.chadd.org

Colorado State Department of Education Twice-Exceptional Students Resource Book—http://www.cde.state.co.us/gt/download/pdf/TwiceExceptionalResourceHandbook.pdf

Council for Exceptional Children—http://www.cec.sped.org

Dyscalculia (math learning disability)—http://www.dyscalculia.org

Educational Research & Information Center (ERIC)—http://www.ericec.org

Gifted Development Center—http://www.gifteddevelopment.com

The Gifted With Learning Differences Educational Network—http://www.gtldnetwork.org

GTLDNet—http://www.gtldnet.org

GT World—http://www.gtworld.org

Hoagies' Gifted Education—http://www.hoagiesgifted.org

International Dyslexia Society—http://interdys.org

LD Online—http://www.ldonline.org

Learning Ally (formally Recording for the Blind and Dyslexic)—http://www.LearningAlly.org

Learning Disabilities Association of America—http://www.ldanatl.org

National Association for Gifted Children—http://www.nagc.org

National Center for Learning Disabilities—http://www.ncld.org

National Dissemination Center for Children With Disabilities—http://www.nichcy.org

NLD on the Web!—http://www.nldontheweb.org

Nonverbal Learning Disorders Association—http://www.nlda.org

Parent Encouragement Program—http://www.parentencouragement.org

Schwab Learning—http://www.SchwabLearning.org

ThinkFun—http://www.thinkfun.com

Uniquely Gifted—http://www.uniquelygifted.org

Wrightslaw Libraries—http://www.wrightslaw.com

REFERENCES

2E Newsletter. (n.d.). *2e resources: Schools and programs for 2e students.* Retrieved from http://www.2enewsletter.com/topic_resources_schools-programs.html

Abeel, S. (1994). *Reach for the moon.* Middleton, WI: Pfeifer-Hamilton.

Administrators and Staff of Bridges Academy. (2011, September). Writing and 2e Learner: Issues and Strategies: Anxiety. *2e: Twice Exceptional Newsletter*, 3–6.

American Psychiatric Association. (2000). *Diagnostic and statistical manual of mental disorders* (4th ed., Text rev.). Washington, DC: Author.

American Psychiatric Association. (2013a). *Diagnostic and statistical manual of mental disorders* (5th ed.). Washington, DC: Author.

American Psychiatric Association. (2013b). *Highlights of changes from DSM-IV-TR to DSM-5*. Washington, DC: Author. Retrieved from http://www.psychiatry.org/dsm5

Americans with Disabilities Act, 42 U.S.C. §§ 12102 et seq. (1990).

Americans with Disabilities Amendments Act, Pub. Law 110–325 (September 25, 2008).

Barnes-Robinson, L., Jeweler, S., & Ricci, M. C. (2004, June). Potential: Winged possibilities to dreams realized! *Parenting for High Potential*, 20–25.

Barnes-Robinson, L., Ricci, M. C. & Jeweler, S. (2009, December). Pathways for developing potential in the social-emotional realm. *Parenting for High Potential*, 11–17.

Barton, J. M., & Starnes, W. T. (1989). Identifying distinguishing characteristics of gifted and talented/learning disabled students. *Roeper Review, 12,* 23–29.

Baum, S. (1984). Meeting the needs of gifted learning disabled students. *Roeper Review, 7,* 16–19.

Baum, S. (1990). *Gifted but learning disabled: A puzzling paradox*. Reston, VA: Council for Exceptional Children. (ERIC Document Reproduction Service No. ED321484)

Baum, S. (2004). *Twice-exceptional and special populations of gifted students*. Thousand Oaks, CA: Corwin Press.

Baum, S., Cooper, C., Neu, T., & Owen, S. V. (1997). *Evaluation of Project High Hopes (Project R206A30159-95)*. Washington, DC: U.S. Department of Education.

Baum, S., Emerick, L., Herman, G., & Dixon, J. (1989). Identification, programs and enrichment strategies for gifted learning disabled youth. *Roeper Review, 12,* 48–53.

Baum, S., Owen, S. V., & Dixon, J. (1991). *To be gifted and learning disabled*. Waco, TX: Prufrock Press.

Bloom, B. (Ed.). (1956). *Taxonomy of educational objectives: The classification of educational goals. Handbook I: Cognitive domain*. New York, NY: Longmans Green.

Brody, L. E., & Mills, C. J. (1997). Gifted children with learning disabilities: A review of the issues. *Journal of Learning Disabilities, 30,* 282–297.

Burton, J., Horowitz, R., & Abeles, H. (1999). Learning in and through the arts: Curriculum implications. In T. Fisk (Ed.),

Champions of change. Washington, DC: Arts Education Partnership.

Chen, G. (2007). *What is a charter school?* Retrieved from http://www.publicschoolreview.com/articles/3

Cline, S., & Schwartz, D. (1999). *Diverse populations of gifted children.* Englewood Cliffs, NJ: Merrill/Prentice Hall.

Coleman, M. R. (2003). *The identification of students who are gifted.* Washington, DC: Gifted Education Digests. (ERIC EC Digest #E644)

Colorado State Department of Education. (2009). *Twice-exceptional students: Gifted students with learning disabilities* (2nd ed.). Retrieved from http://www.cde.state.co.us/gt/download/pdf/twiceexceptionalresourcehandbook.pdf

Council for Exceptional Children. (2000). *Making assessment accommodations: A toolkit for educators.* Reston, VA: Author.

Dabrowski, K. (1964). *Positive disintegration.* Boston, MA: Little Brown.

de Bono, E. (1986). *Six thinking hats.* New York, NY: Little Brown.

Dix, J., & Schafer, S. (1996). From paradox to performance. *Gifted Child Today, 19,* 22–29.

Durheim, M. (2012). *Hot topics in Section 504: Frequently asked questions.* Retrieved from http://www.region10.org/Dyslexia/Documents/HotTopicsin504-FAQ8-2012-HandoutMaryDurheim.pdf

Dweck, C. (2010). Mind-sets and equitable education. *Principal Leadership, 10,* 5, 26–29.

Education Center. (n.d.). *504 plans vs. IEP.* Retrieved from http://www.ed-center.com/504

Eide, F., & Eide, B. (n.d.). *Underachievement.* Retrieved from http://www.neurolearning.com/underachieve.htm

Fisk, T. B. (Ed.). (1999). *Champions of change.* Washington, DC: Arts Education Partnership.

Friend, M. (1996). *The power of two: Making a difference through co-teaching.* Port Chester, NY: National Educational Resources.

Fuchs, D. (2009). *What is the relationship between RtI and special education?* Retrieved from http://www.rti4success.org/

askthexpert/what-relationship-between-rti-and-special-education-december-2009-0409

Fuchs, L. S., Fuchs, D., Eaton, S. B., Hamlett, C., & Karns, K. (2000). Supplementing teacher judgments of mathematics test accommodations with objective data sources. *School Psychology Review, 29*, 65–85.

Gardner, H. (1983). *Frames of mind: The theory of multiple intelligences.* New York, NY: Basic Books.

Hardy, L. (2010). The twice-exceptional child. Schools struggle to help students who are gifted and have learning disabilities, but some are successful. *American School Board Journal, 197*, 24–27.

Higgins, D., Baldwin, L., & Pereles, D. (2000). *Comparison of characteristics of gifted students with or without disabilities.* Unpublished manuscript.

Idaho State Department of Education. (2010). *Twice-exceptional: Students with both gifts and challenges or disabilities.* Retrieved from http://www.sde.idaho.gov/site/gifted_talented/twice-exceptional/docs/2E%20Manual.pdf

Individuals with Disabilities Education Act, 20 U.S.C. §1401 et seq. (1990).

Individuals with Disabilities Education Improvement Act, Pub. Law 108-446 (December 3, 2004).

J. L., M. L., and K. L. v. Mercer Island School District (C06-494P), W. D. Was. (2006).

Jeweler, S., & Barnes-Robinson, L., (1999). Curriculum from a conflict-resolution perspective. *Kappa Delta Pi Record, 35*(3), 112–116.

Klein Independent School District and Texas Education Agency v. Per Hovem, Knut Hovem, and Signe Hovem (10-20694), U.S. Court of Appeals for the Fifth Circuit (2012).

Klotz, M. B., & Canter, A. (2006). *Response to intervention (RTI): A primer for parents.* Retrieved from http://www.nasponline.org/resources/factsheets/rtiprimer.aspx

Kurzweil, R. (1999). *The age of spiritual machines: When computers exceed human intelligence.* New York, NY: Penguin.

Landrum, T. J. (1989). Gifted and learning disabled students: Practical considerations for teachers. *Academic Therapy, 24,* 533–545.

Lenz, K., & Schumaker, J. (1999). *Adapting language arts, social studies, and science materials for the inclusive classroom: Volume 3: Grades six through eight.* Reston, VA: Council for Exceptional Children.

Logsdon, A. (2011). *Help for all kids with response to intervention.* Retrieved from http://www.learningdisabilities.about.com/od/disabilitylaws/a/rtiforldkids.html

Maryland State Department of Education. (1999). *Maryland state performance assessment program.* Baltimore, MD: Author.

Maryland State Department of Education. (2000). *Requirements for accommodating, excusing, and exempting students in Maryland assessment programs.* Baltimore, MD: Author.

Maryland State Department of Education. (2001). *Identifying specific learning disabilities.* Baltimore, MD: Author.

Maryland Task Force on Gifted and Talented Education. (1994). *Renewing our commitment to the education of gifted and talented students: An essential component of educational reform.* Baltimore, MD: Maryland State Department of Education.

McAlpine, J., Weincek, B., Jeweler, S., & Finkbinder, M. (1982). *CPS: Planning new worlds.* New York, NY: Sunburst Communications.

McAlpine, J., Weincek, B., Jeweler, S., & Finkbinder, F. (2011). *Understanding India.* Hawthorne, NJ: Educational Impressions.

McTighe, J., & Wiggins, G. (1999). *The understanding by design handbook.* Alexandra, VA: Association for Supervision and Curriculum Development.

Monroe, S. J. (2007). *Dear colleague letter: Access by students with disabilities to challenging academic programs.* Retrieved from http://www2.ed.gov/about/offices/list/ocr/letters/colleague-20071226.html

Montgomery County Public Schools. (1994). *Conflict resolution tools: Elementary version, teaching through the curriculum.* Rockville, MD: Author.

Mooney, J., & Cole, D. (2000). *Learning outside the lines: Two Ivy League students with learning disabilities and ADHD give you the tools for academic success and educational revolution.* New York, NY: Fireside.

Mr. and Mrs. I. vs Maine School Administrative District No. 55, 04-165-P-H (U.S. District Court, Maine, 2006).

Musgrove, M. (2011). *A Response to Intervention (RTI) process cannot be used to delay-deny an evaluation for eligibility under the Individuals with Disabilities Education Act (IDEA).* Retrieved from http://www.rti4success.org/pdf/RTI%20 Memo_1-21-11r.pdf

National Association for Gifted Children. (1998). *Students with concomitant gifts and learning disabilities.* Washington, DC: Author.

National Association for Gifted Children. (2008a). *Redefining giftedness for a new century: Shifting the paradigm.* Washington, DC: Author.

National Association for Gifted Children. (2008b). *The role of assessments in the identification of gifted students.* Washington, DC: Author.

National Association for Gifted Children. (2010). *NAGC Pre-K–Grade 12 Gifted Programming Standards: A blueprint for quality gifted education programs.* Washington, DC: Author.

National Education Association. (2006). *The twice-exceptional dilemma.* Washington, DC: Author.

Neumann, L. C. (2010). *Don't get caught in the lazy trap.* Retrieved from http://www.2e newsletter.com/article_lazy_trap.html

No Child Left Behind Act, 20 U.S.C. §6301 (2001).

Pace, J. (2008, Jan. 11). *Finding the twice exceptional: Identifying bright students with learning difficulties.* Lecture presented at Johns Hopkins University, Baltimore, MD.

Piechowski, M. M. (1991). Emotional development and emotional giftedness. In N. Colangelo & G. Davis (Eds.), *Handbook of gifted education* (pp. 285–306) Boston, MA: Allyn & Bacon.

Posny, A. (2010). *This is in response to your letters . . .* (Letter). Retrieved from http://www2.ed.gov/policy/speced/guid/idea/letters/2010-1/redacteda011310eval1q2010.pdf

Postma, M., Peters, D., Kearney, K., & Gilman, B. (2012). *What parents and educators should know about RtI.* Retrieved from http://nagc.sclivelearningcenter.com/index.aspx?PID=4241&SID=107836

Reardon, M. (2009). *Response to intervention and gifted and talented education.* Retrieved from http://www.opi.mt.gov/pub/RTI/Resources/RTI_Gifted_Talented.pdf

Reis, S. M., & McCoach, D. B. (2000). The underachievement of gifted students: What do we know and where do we go? *Gifted Child Quarterly, 44,* 152–170.

Renzulli, J. S. (1977). *The enrichment triad model: A guide for developing defensible programs for the gifted and talented.* Waco, TX: Prufrock Press.

Renzulli, J. S., & Reis, S. M. (1997). *The schoolwide enrichment model: A how-to guide for educational excellence* (2nd ed.). Waco, TX: Prufrock Press.

Roeper, A., & Higgins, A. (2007). *The "I" of the beholder: A guided journey to the essence of a child.* Scottsdale, AZ: Great Potential Press.

Rose, D. H., & Gravel, J. W. (2010). Universal design for learning. In E. Baker, P. Peterson, & B. McGaw (Eds.), *International encyclopedia of education* (3rd ed., pp. 119–124). Oxford, England: Elsevier.

Samuels, C. A. (2008). Response to Intervention sparks interest, questions. *Education Week, 27*(20), 1. Retrieved from http://www.edweek.org/ew/articles/2008/01/23/20rtireact.h27.html

Section 504 of the Rehabilitation Act, 29 U.S.C. Section 706 et. seq. (1973).

Shevitz, B., Weinfeld, R., Jeweler, S., & Barnes-Robinson, L. (2003) Mentoring empowers gifted/learning disabled students to soar. *Roeper Review, 26,* 37–40.

Shevitz, B. R., Stemple, M., Barnes-Robinson, L., & Jeweler, S. (2011). *101 school success tools for smart kids with learning difficulties.* Waco, TX Prufrock Press.

Silver, L. (2012, January/February). Déjà vu—all over again! *LDA Newsbriefs, 47*, 1, 4.

Silverman, L. K. (1989). Invisible gifts, invisible handicaps. *Roeper Review, 12,* 37–41.

Silverman, S., Iseman, J., & Jeweler, S. (2009). *School success for kids with ADHD.* Waco, TX: Prufrock Press.

Silverman, S., & Weinfeld, R. (2007). *School success for kids with Asperger's syndrome.* Waco, TX: Prufrock Press.

St. Edward's University. (n.d.). *Enabling versus empowering.* Retrieved from http://www.stedwards.edu/cte/resources/enabling.htm

Starnes, W., Ginevan, J., Stokes, L., & Barton, J. (1988, March). *A study in the identification, differential diagnosis, and remediation of underachieving highly able students.* Paper presented at annual meeting of the Council for Exceptional Children, Washington, DC.

Thurlow, M., House, A., Scott, D., & Ysseldyke, J. (2001). *State participation and accommodation policies for students with disabilities.* Minneapolis, MN: National Center for Educational Outcomes.

Tindal, G., & Fuchs, L. (1999). *A summary of research on test changes: An empirical basis for defining accommodations.* Lexington, KY: MidSouth Regional Resource Center.

Title IV, Part B. [Jacob K. Javits Gifted and Talented Students Education Act of 1988], Elementary and Secondary Education Act of 1988, 20 U.S.C. 3061 et seq.

Tomlinson, C. A. (1999). *The differentiated classroom: Responding to the needs of all learners.* Alexandria, VA: ASCD.

Tomlinson, C. A. (2000). *Differentiation of instruction in the elementary grades.* Reston, VA: ERIC Clearinghouse on Disabilities and Gifted Education. (ERIC Document Reproduction Service No. ED443572)

VanTassel-Baska, J. (2007). *Alternative assessments with gifted and talented students.* Waco, TX: Prufrock Press.

VanTassel-Baska, J. (1991). Serving the disabled gifted through educational collaboration. *Journal for the Education of the Gifted, 14,* 246–266.

Weinfeld, R., Barnes-Robinson, L., Jeweler, S., & Shevitz, B. (2002). Academic programs for gifted and talented/learning disabled students. *Roeper Review, 24,* 226–233.

Weinfeld, R., & Davis, M. (2008). *Special needs advocacy resource book.* Waco, TX Prufrock Press.

West, T. G. (1991). *In the mind's eye: Visual thinkers, gifted people with learning difficulties, computer images, and the ironies of creativity.* Buffalo, NY: Prometheus Books.

West Chester Area School District v. Chad C., 194 F.sup.2d 417 (E.D.Pa.2002).

Whitmore, J. R. (1980). *Giftedness, conflict, and underachievement.* Boston, MA: Allyn & Bacon.

Whitmore, J. R. (1981). Gifted children with handicapping conditions: A new frontier. *Exceptional Children, 48,* 106–113.

Willard-Holt, C. (1999, May). *Dual exceptionalities* (ERIC EC Digest #574). Reston, VA: ERIC Clearinghouse on Disabilities and Gifted Education.

ABOUT THE AUTHORS

Rich Weinfeld received his master's degree from Trinity College and is certified in early childhood and elementary education, special education, administration, and supervision. He has long been an advocate for quality educational programs for all students. Twenty-six years of his 30-year career with Montgomery County Public Schools were spent in a variety of leadership roles in special education. He has expertise in working with students with a wide range of disabilities, including learning disabilities, autism spectrum disorders, and emotional disturbance. He served as Montgomery County's first full-time coordinator of programs for students who are simultaneously gifted and learning disabled (GTLD). His books include *Smart Kids with Learning Difficulties: Overcoming Obstacles and Realizing Potential*, *Helping Boys Succeed in School*, *School Success* *for Kids With Asperger's Syndrome*, and *Special Needs Advocacy Resource Book*. He was co-host of a weekly Internet radio show, "Teach Your Children Well: Hot Topics in Education," on http://www.voiceamerica.com. He has been selected to present at numerous national conferences, been an instructor at Johns Hopkins University, and served on the board of directors for the Association for Educators of Gifted Underachieving Student (AEGUS). Rich directs Weinfeld Education Group, LLC, a group of nearly 50 educational consultants, psychologists, neuropsychologists, behavior intervention specialists, and other direct service providers. In addition to his advocacy work, he does extensive parent and staff training and consults with schools about appropriate programming for all students. More information about his endeavors can be found at http://www.richweinfeld.com

Sue Jeweler, a retired teacher, spent her 30-year career in Maryland's Montgomery County Public Schools. Sue has been a consultant to the John F. Kennedy Center for the Performing Arts, the Smithsonian Institution, National Geographic Society, Berns & Kay, and Street Law. Her expertise has been used in a variety of projects with an outreach to teachers nationally and internationally. She has coauthored two educational kits, numerous journal articles, and more than 40 books including the acclaimed *Smart Kids with Learning Difficulties: Overcoming Obstacles and Realizing Potential* and *School Success for Kids with ADHD*. Sue, an award-winning educator, is the recipient of the prestigious *Washington Post* Agnes Meyer Outstanding Teaching Award. She is listed in *Who's Who Among America's Teachers, Who's Who of American Women*, and the *International Who's Who*. She coestablished Creative Family Projects, LLC, which identifies problems and provides solutions by synthesizing information from organizations, institutions, and corporations into booklets and training modules for the benefit of children, youth, and families. Her most recent project is the coauthored booklet, *Mommies and Daddies in Jail*.

Linda Barnes-Robinson has worked in gifted education for more than 30 years, and has devoted her professional life to advocating for children and families. With Montgomery County Public Schools, she coordinated the identification of gifted and talented students, advocated for parents and students, and worked to establish one of the first comprehensive programs for gifted/learning disabled students in the nation. She is a nationally recognized trainer and educational consultant in gifted identification, conflict resolution and mediation, and gifted/learning disabled programs. She has coauthored and edited numerous articles, manuals, books, and curricula documents. Her most recent book, *101 School Success Tools for Smart Kids With Learning Difficulties,* provides field-tested tools for parents and teachers. She received her bachelor's degree from Cedar Crest College, her master's degree from The George Washington University, and a postgraduate certificate in family mediation from The Catholic University of America.

Betty Roffman Shevitz has more than 30 years of experience with gifted students. She currently serves as an instructional specialist for gifted students in Montgomery County Schools and is responsible for the screening and identification of students for seven centers for the highly gifted. In addition, she coordinates the Wings Mentor Program, a countywide program that she codeveloped to support students who are both gifted and learning disabled. Over the years, she has directed her attention to special populations, dedicated to helping nurture students' potential. She has extensive experience both in the classroom and in the central office of school districts with large populations of gifted students. She was involved in the initial year of a program designed for identifying and nurturing gifted students in underserved populations. She has developed curriculum, presented at national and state conferences, and served as an educational consultant and a teacher trainer. She is coauthor of *101 School Success Tools for Smart Kids With Learning Difficulties* (2011), *Smart Kids With Learning Difficulties: Overcoming Obstacles and Realizing Potential* (2006), and various articles, including "Academic Programs for Gifted and Talented/Learning Disabled Students" (2002) and "Mentoring Empowers Gifted/Learning Disabled Students to Soar" (2003). Betty received her bachelor's degree in education and her master's degree in Gifted Education from the University of Virginia.

For more information, or to contact the authors, visit http://www.smartkidsresource.com.

Printed in the United States
by Baker & Taylor Publisher Services